TERRY WOLFE

GOD'S FAULT

BOOK 1

THE PARADOX OF FUNDAMENTALISM

The Paradox of Fundamentalism

God's Fault, Book 1

Copyright © 2023 by Terry Wolfe

Contact: maybewrong@protonmail.com

All Bible quotations have been reworded unless a specific translation is mentioned. Rewording was based on the author's review of multiple English translations, attempting to find the best balance of clarity and readability.

CONTENTS

PREFACE

Welcome to the first book of the *God's Fault* series.

God willing, this will be the first of many installments exploring the paradox of Reality in light of an Almighty God. We begin with the paradox of the Bible itself, as well as those who champion it most proudly and directly – that is, the fundamentalists. To them, the Bible is supposed to be God's Word, the guide to all important truth, and the ultimate weapon against delusion; but paradoxically, it has also been the source of many deranged beliefs, and few can peer through its mysteries to arrive at a fair interpretation. We must examine what it means to be a self-proclaimed "Bible-believer", and how to deal with the controversies embedded in our favorite holy book.

Some don't even realize the Bible is a compilation of ancient texts written over many centuries by many different people, in three different languages, translated by many people and bound together into a self-contained library. The question of language and cultural context is important to understanding these old scriptures, but the fundamentalist tends to oversimplify the idea of the Bible. In this book we will not only acknowledge what's wrong about such simple assumptions, but ask what it means to the modern believer to invest in writings so far removed from the original authors and their culture.

With this series, my goal is simple: *I want to reduce cognitive dissonance in Christian worship.* "Cognitive dissonance" is a psychology term for what happens when a person's preferred beliefs are contradicted by reality. Studies (and common sense) have proven that people refuse to acknowledge when such contradictions exist, denying unpleasant facts rather than reformulating their beliefs. We all experience cognitive dissonance to some extent, but when it comes to religion it's especially dangerous to leave it unchecked. A great danger exists, because cognitive dissonance does not create a sense of shame about being in error, but rather a sense of pride. People love their delusion, and try to convert others to believe the same things in order to surround themselves with people who won't judge them, and instead support and reinforce their error. Dissonance therefore has its own evangelism, becoming like yeast (or "leaven") which spreads on its own and multiplies.

> *Your boasting is not good. Do you not realize that a little leaven leavens the whole lump?*
>
> *(1 Corinthians 5:8)*

How much cognitive dissonance is in the church by now? In this series I hope to explore the full breadth, although things have gotten so extreme that I wonder if any person can catalog even half of it. Many are unwilling to face the facts about God, the Bible, and human history, to the point where we are in danger of promoting a counterfeit Christianity.

I am concerned about offending weak Christians. Paul tells us to avoid doing things that would offend ignorant believers,[1] acknowledging that, even if they are misguided, it is more important to support them than give them a reason to doubt. He also explains that not all believers are ready for "meat", but must be given "milk"[2] until they're ready. However, Paul was writing to brand-new Christians in an era when there was no "Bible" at all – just Old Testament writings and a new handful of letters that were still being written and spread around. These were pagan converts who had never been trained in Christian thought, giving up their entire civilization's history and identity in order to learn a strange new doctrine about how to live. We're in a very different time period today, and I think we are more in need of this warning given by Jesus Christ to the churches:

> *"Because you say, 'I am wealthy and have become rich, and need nothing,' but you do not realize that you are wretched, pitiful, poor, blind, and naked, I advise you to buy from me gold refined by fire, so that you may become rich; white garments so that you may be clothed and your shameful nakedness not be exposed; and salve to anoint your eyes so that you may see clearly. Those whom I love, I also rebuke and discipline. Therefore, be zealous and repent."*
>
> *(Revelation 2:17-19)*

This warning is about overconfidence. Fundamentalists have been plagued by this problem, not because they reject the Bible, but because they talk so arrogantly about it. Rather than doing research and learning how to defend it with reason and evidence, they shut out arguments and let cognitive dissonance

---

1   Romans 14 is entirely about this topic.
2   1 Corinthians 3:2

shield them from the controversies. The result is a steady descent into childish doctrines. Churches have specialized in protecting their members from the deeper truths, always catering to the lowest common denominator, never challenging the theology of the simpleminded, and promoting a childlike faith with milk instead of training warriors with meat.

Maybe we're all getting a little tired of milk, however. In my experience of teaching the Bible, people have been very receptive to a more mature approach to difficult questions related to God and Scripture. If we don't tackle these topics, fake experts and cults will. A willingness to tackle these subjects not only helps clear away cognitive dissonance, but shows outsiders that their concerns are valid but not impossible to address. Hiding from them won't do any good.

We must face up to the real Almighty God, who treats this world as His footstool.[3] It is nonsensical to sing His praises while simultaneously turning a blind eye to His judgments. My aim is to align the reader with a more stark and unapologetic view of God. Yes, I say "unapologetic", even though I must lament His choices before I can defend them. Others act as if they are defending Him by pretending He is somebody else altogether! To me, honoring a false version of the true God is akin to serving a false god. That is idolatry. Ultimately, I will conclude this series with a theory that defends God's decisions as being just and righteous, but it is only after we eliminate cognitive dissonance, so that we can see what kind of God we are supposed to revere.

---

3   (Isaiah 66:1) *Thus the LORD says: "The heavens are my throne and the earth serves as my footstool. Where then is the house you will build for me? Where is the place that I will rest?"*

It will be necessary for me to wade deeply into uncomfortable territory and speak rather audaciously. Having already established some of my beliefs in my previous books, I feel comfortable continuing to overturn traditional assumptions for the sake of getting nearer to (what I believe is) an authentic relationship with the God of Israel. To Jesus Christ belongs all praise, power, and recognition, unto the glory of the Father. However, in keeping with the premise of this series, I should add: to Him belongs all *accountability* as well.

INTRODUCTION

I WRITE THIS BOOK in grief for my brothers and sisters who have reached out to God for answers but found only uncertainty. I can think of nothing more tragic, because we know that our lives are but an opportunity to learn how to please God before the Judgment. Many scholars and intellectuals have argued that the "Problem of Evil" is one of the greatest controversies of theology, but they're all wrong. The Problem of Evil states that an all-knowing, all-powerful God can't exist, because if He is all-knowing and all-powerful He would never allow Evil to exist and thrive; therefore, they say, He must either not know everything, or not be able to stop it. And although this paradox has bothered theologians for thousands of years, it is one of the dumbest arguments I've ever heard. Indeed, despite the premise of this series being about God's accountability for the problems of mankind, *God's Fault* will not at all bother to waste time on it at length. The so-called paradox can resolved in two words: Judgment Day.

All evil and good will be dealt with on that day, so that every individual soul will meet its Maker and be given a verdict that is unquestionably righteous. The eternal wages of good and evil will more than make up for any fleeting sense of injustice we may experience in this short life. Theologians somehow ignore the Judgment Day's balancing effect; frankly, they become fools, not taking the Word of God seriously enough. They are like little children who speak endlessly without knowing what they say, underestimating God. A fundamentalist believes that Judgment Day is real, and live accordingly. Their theology acknowledges that it ought to re-organize the priorities of every last human being. But for this very reason, it is not evil itself that should logically bother us, but the paradoxical path to pleasing God.

Learning how to please God is the best thing a person can attain in life, and separation from God is worse than any suffering we could experience. Think about it rationally. For as bad as physical torment may feel, it only affects the body, coming and going and ultimately vanishing with our body's demise. And while emotional suffering (such as betrayal, isolation, and humiliation) can leave lasting scars on our hearts, these also edify us by showing us to turn to God for hope, not man. If we truly believe what the Bible tells us, it would be more enviable to be a tortured prisoner who owns nothing but the crown of Salvation, than a ruler of nations whom God despises! Seeking God's wisdom is the most urgent priority in life, and to ignore Him is the greatest folly.

> *Wisdom is supreme, so acquire wisdom; and, of all the things you may obtain, obtain understanding!*
>
> *(Proverbs 4:7)*

We know how to acquire wisdom, because the Bible tells us plainly in many places:

And He said to mankind: Behold, the fear of the Lord is wisdom, and to turn away from evil is understanding.

(Job 28:28)

The fear of the LORD is the beginning of wisdom; all who follow His precepts gain a wealth of understanding.

(Psalms 111:10)

The fear of the LORD is the beginning of wisdom, but fools despise wisdom and discipline.

(Proverbs 1:7)

The fear of the LORD is the beginning of wisdom, and knowledge of the Holy One is understanding.

(Proverbs 9:10)

Amen! But now we see the real problem, and the reason why millions of self-professed believers are struggling to understand the Bible and have a meaningful relationship with God: we can't fear God if we don't have an honest appraisal of Him. As long as we cling to a false version of God, we cannot fear the real Almighty and gain real wisdom. It would be like a child trying to respect their father, but mistaking a stranger for their father; the honor they give to the stranger is worthless. First there must be a recognition of the real Father.

And again, speaking of priorities, the Apostle Paul gives us a wonderful reminder of what matters in life when he recounts his many misfortunes this way:

What an incredible statement! Most of us can hardly imagine losing everything we have, but if we lose it in the pursuit of Jesus Christ we are really exchanging it for an eternal reward. That's what a fundamentalist would say, at least. And that's why we should have all the more sympathy for those who seek God but do not find Him. As I said, nothing is more tragic.

Due to their irrational devotion to the Bible, fundamentalists are the best and noblest of all the faithful, in theory. They want an intimate familiarity with the text, and no middle men to twist its meaning. They say the Bible is not only sacred in the generic sense of being important and off-limits to tampering, but rather, a divinely-authored story meant for all of mankind to hear. This belief has carried the Good Book farther than any other form of worship. Fundamentalists are the ones who enjoy saying things like, "B.I.B.L.E. stands for Basic Instructions Before Leaving Earth". The most extreme kind of fundamentalist has no fear of mankind, nor of death itself, but lays down his very life for the Scriptures, knowing that there is no cause more worthy and that his reward is secure in heaven. The simplicity and beauty of such teachings, matched by a long and impressive history of martyrdom, ought to inspire courage and boldness in every believer. I have counted myself as a fundamentalist to the fullest extent, and I thank God that I was raised in such a tradition, as a Mennonite; a people whose doctrinal forefathers were hunted through forests and ravines, imprisoned in dungeons, and tortured mercilessly for their unwavering adherence to the Word of God. But there are other kinds of fundamentalists out there, and they don't all see eye-to-eye. We will explore these differences to show how a shared struggle to embody its teachings proves that the text fails to produce clarity and consistency.

LOVED ONES WILL DIE, money will evaporate, and our accomplishments will be nullified by others. Woe to those who believe otherwise! However, because we know life is ephemeral, our paradox becomes all the more galling – namely, that the Bible often disorients the very people who depend on it for hope. If we think of the Bible as a key that unlocks the door to truth, it seems to be bent, so that it won't fit in the hole and give us access. Of all the tragedies the Lord has inflicted on mankind, blinding the eyes of those who desire the Truth is the cruelest.

Ah, but I have spoken foolishly already, by implicating God in the destruction of man. May He forgive me! In this series I must speak as a great fool, because I sit astonished at His feet, not understanding the tragedy of the paradox. I refuse to deny the tragedy's existence, because I cannot afford cognitive dissonance, but I also cannot doubt the infinite goodness of my God. And so I sit as a fool, and speak foolishly about my sorrow. Forgive me for this, reader. Perhaps by the end of this book you will see the paradox too, and fear God for creating it.

If you have no love your fellow man it may be easy to dismiss the paradox of the Bible's failure to instruct mankind. But Christ commanded us to love one another, so how can we ignore it? Billions of humans are wandering to their deaths in ignorance, despite the Bible being the most popular book in the world.

Some of you will shift the blame to the individual who stumbles, as if they ought to know how to navigate the surprising controversies of the text by instinct; or as if you are immune to these controversies yourself! Wiser readers might not dismiss the problem altogether, but only insist that knowledge about controversies is irrelevant, because we are commanded only to love our neighbors, etc. and in any case, we are saved by faith alone, etc. Very well said! But there is still confusion and ignorance everywhere, leading men to doom. And the Bible is still under attack, which calls for a defense, and its supposed defenders do not answer properly. Reassuring ourselves about faith while closing our eyes and ears is not really faith, but dissonance. And I know someone else will assert that the Bible is flawless, no matter what people say, even without looking into the criticisms. But must we defend our faith by going into denial? Our own Bible says to seek insights and understanding above all! Let's not be hypocrites. If there is one thing profitable in this lifetime, it is a genuine search of the Holy Bible, but much like worshiping God, we must be honest about it.

I think some Christians are ready to pledge loyalty to the Bible on one hand while abandoning it to Satan on the other. This is not virtue. It shows no regard for the lost sheep who need their Shepherd and have been ensnared by arguments along the way. We can help dismantle the traps and set them free, but we have to acknowledge what's really going on.

Too many have defended the Bible ignorantly, including myself. In the process, I am afraid we are making a mockery of it. I ask you, is that the best we can do to honor God? Does He want to be worshiped by sycophants and cowards who mouth prayers and sing hymns while turning a blind eye to controversies, or suppress their discomfort? Is He pleased by sermons of men who delicately tiptoe around His judgments, as if to avoid knocking Him over and shattering Him like a piece of fine pottery? Wasn't it our God who chose Moses as his friend, although he argued with Him often and questioned His decisions? Wasn't it the Angel of God who spoke thusly (Gen 32:28): *"Your name will no longer be Jacob, but instead Israel, because you have fought with God and with man, and have endured."* God chose for His people a man so stubborn that he wrestled with God's presence all night for no reason, and afterward had the audacity to cling to Him for a blessing! And when Jesus met the skeptic who doubted whether anything good could come from Nazareth, he did not rebuke him, but said (John 1:47): *"Behold, a true Jew, in whom there is no deceit!"*

Perhaps God is amused by a man who dares to face up to Him and acknowledge the absurdity of our situation, while still trusting Him. And it is absurd, make no mistake. Some will say that speaking against God is to condemn your own soul. Perhaps so, but the love of our fellow man compels us to cry out anyway, for the sake of the doomed, to acknowledge the trouble of our condition and plead for help. Can we cry for help while we deny a problem? And can we acknowledge a problem without admitting that God could have prevented it?

BUT WHAT PARADOX? WHAT condition? Who is doomed? Let the reader survey the world's condition. Greater men than you and I have lamented its doom in the past: all the prophets, the saints, and the Lord himself were touched with sorrow for this world, because they recognized the souls headed for oblivion. They had their own scoffers, who also turned a blind eye to the crisis. Our present world is going to Hell, and time is running out. What can be done about it? Can any of us turn the tide? If the answer is to worship the true God, so that we shine as a guiding beacon to others (as we find in Mat 5:14), then we must hurry to realign our notion of God with Reality.

If the best way to please God is to be a fundamentalist, then the situation is grim. Not only do very few fit this category, but fundamentalists have their own problems, which we must explore in this book. Perhaps these problems can be overcome, but first we must understand what we're up against. We cannot rid ourselves of cognitive dissonance by fundamentalist confidence alone. Let me grieve this fact! This book contains the words of a tired man who has no other way to express his dismay. I hope there is still time to present not only the problem, but a possible solution, by the time this series is finished. As of today, I still have the right, as a Canadian who is protected by the Canadian Charter of Rights and Freedoms, Section 2(a), to speak about these things freely. It guarantees Freedom of Religion, which it defines this way: *"the right to entertain such religious beliefs as a person chooses, the right to declare religious beliefs openly and without fear of hindrance or reprisal, and the right to manifest religious belief by worship and practise or by teaching and dissemination."* This is precisely what I will be doing in this book.

Let me also state emphatically that I am not an expert on anything, and I have never been educated properly. I have written two books on religion so far, *Maybe Everyone Is Wrong: Revelations, Conspiracy, and the Kingdom of Heaven*, and its follow-up, *Fire In The Rabbit Hole*. Here, I will not put forward a particular hypothesis, as I did in those books, but I must again speculate on many things out of ignorance. I have consulted many experts in one form or another, and I've done as much research as I could, but it is the very confidence of experts that robs me of my own. Their weak arguments, condescension, arrogance, and assumptions only testify to the magnitude of the true crisis. God help us!

Rather than positing a theory, I put forward a question: *why does it have to be this way, God? Is this the best You could do to help the helpless? What is the Divine reason behind all of this disputation?*

THE DEVIL IN THE DETAILS

THE BIBLE IS DANGEROUS, but the Devil is not afraid of it. We are told it is like a very sharp sword:

> *The Word of God is alive and active. It is sharper than any double-edged sword, so that it is able to divide the soul from the spirit, and the joint from the marrow; all the way to the desires and thoughts of the heart.*
>
> *(Hebrews 4:12)*

To Christian preachers, this "sharpness" enables them to "cut to the heart of the matter" and convict people of their sins, showing them the need for repentance and forgiveness. But the Bible can be just as powerful in the wrong hands. When somebody twists God's Word, it can corrupt, blind, and destroy the understanding of the ignorant, and this seems to be the job of the Devil.

If, as the fundamentalist believes, the Devil is an actual entity out there somewhere in the world, having existed since at least the earliest days of Creation, then we should always be watchful for his schemes. He is the inventor of deception:

> *You belong to your father, the Devil, and your will is to do what your father wants. He was a murderer from the beginning, and does not stand in the Truth, because there is no truth in him. When he lies, he speaks out of his own character, for he is a liar, and <u>the father of lies</u>.*
>
> *(John 8:44)*

Jesus spoke these words to his doubters, pointing out that they belonged to their father, the Devil, because they refused to acknowledge him as the Messiah. Yet although he called them liars, he nonetheless validated their culture's concept of a spiritual arch-villain character called the Devil who was the original rebel against God.

The New Testament clearly portrays the Devil as a real and central figure in the cosmic story of good and evil. But scholars say such a figure was a late Jewish tradition, citing a lack of detail about an evil mastermind in the Old Testament. They have a point, because the "character" of the Devil if much more fleshed out in later writings. Yet fundamentalists point to Zechariah 3:1, where Satan is shown to be accusing Joshua the High Priest in heaven, as well as 1 Chronicles 21:1, when Satan incites David to take a census of Israel. And of course we have the Book of Job, where Satan is portrayed as a roaming inspector who criticizes God's Creation, as Job unfortunately gets dragged into the middle of their debate. To a fundamentalist these passages are proof enough that the Devil has always been real, but scholars scoff at the idea that Job is really an ancient legend from the land of Uz as it purports, and wouldn't even humor the idea that it's anything but poetry.

In Hebrew, "satan" is both a verb and a noun, and it means opposition, or an adversary. The same word is used to describe the Angel of the Lord (in Numbers 22:22) as a noun when he stands in the road, blocking the prophet Balaam. In other places, it's applied to humans, such as 2 Samuel 19:22, when the sons of Zeruiah stand in opposition to David. It therefore cannot be a proper title of a single entity who keeps meddling with God's plans, even if it does get used that way in some places. As for Job's significance, even the Jews of antiquity categorized Job as literature, counting it among their "writings" (*ketuvim*) alongside the poetry of Psalms and Proverbs.[4] Zechariah was likewise a post-Babylon prophet, and we know that 1 and 2 Chronicles (which were a single document split into two parts) were also written after this period, because they reference the edict of Cyrus the Great, who liberated Israel from Babylon. Therefore, even the explanation of David being tempted by "Satan" is not contemporary with the event itself, but a post-Babylon explanation of what happened long before. It's possible that the Jewish concept of this unique Satan figure was developed during the Babylonian exile, as they absorbed ideas from their surrounding captor's culture.

But whether the tradition was late or early, statements by Jesus Christ and the New Testament ought to settle the matter, right? If the fundamentalist outlook is correct, the descriptions of the Devil in the New Testament are not reflective of Jewish traditions, but powerful revelations of the true nature of Reality, which were perhaps concealed in earlier ages. They believe the Devil has been warping the words of the Almighty to suit his own subversive agenda since the earliest days of Man, ensuring that we could never have peace on earth. Why would God allow

---

4   This is also why Protestant Bibles position it immediately before Psalms.

such a devious character to live alongside His Word, or attend Him in heaven to accuse people? Nobody knows. But to this day, the Devil is the one creating falsehoods which ensnare the minds of men and lead them to destruction, subverting God's wishes for all men to be saved.

CONSIDERING THAT MOST PEOPLE will never have a face-to-face encounter with the ultimate spiritual nemesis in their lifetime, I think the phrase "the Devil is in the details" is a more apt warning to give them. Whenever a person reads their Bible and becomes confused about its message, it's almost like the Devil is there, whispering doubts into their ear. And, as the saying implies, it only gets worse as you focus more on details. This is a major paradox of fundamentalism, since they love the Bible so much that they want to know everything about it, but often become disillusioned or afraid when they start hearing from experts. They have to push back against those who are better educated than themselves, driving them into the arms of whatever preacher reassures them.

If the Devil is as ambitious as we are led to believe, he must be attracted to Bible experts. Although the texts are holy, they fail to act as repellent to him. They are more like an invitation. He uses them, finding people in their weakness, and capitalizing on their guilt, selfish impulses, and assumptions. We can look at the temptation of Jesus in the wilderness, where the Devil used Scripture in an attempt to lure Jesus into various mistakes. Jesus rebukes and overcomes the Devil using alternative Scripture, showing that God's Word was critical on both sides. How amazing that even when Christ and the Devil combat, their weapon of choice is Scripture!

But for evil to be so cavalier in using the Word of God is disturbing. It could mean that Christian debates, discussions, and preaching opens new doors for God's enemy to poison the ears of the congregation. Details accomplish this wonderfully, because they can suddenly change the meaning of straightforward passages, or reframe entire stories. They also present contradictions. Fundamentalists do not see the Devil's strategy as an allegory, but a very real spiritual war against real demons who work through false apostles, who are disguised as servants of righteousness. It only makes sense for a fundamentalist to have apprehensions about experts. How many teachings out there in the world are secretly the constructs of the father of lies?

IF DAMNATION AND SALVATION hinge on our ability to conform to God's Word, it's no wonder most of mankind is doomed. However, if someone is cast into Hell, do they go because they failed to seek out the truth, or because the Truth failed to seek them? Do we transform our minds, or are we transformed from above? In light of an Almighty God and a tricky Devil, is man really responsible for his own fate?

Key texts serve as an example of how wording can create problems in unexpected ways:

> *And this is the condemnation: that light is come into the world, and men loved darkness rather than light, because their deeds were evil.*
>
> *(John 3:19)*

This seems like a simple teaching: evil men avoid Jesus because he exposes their deeds, and thus they are condemned. But, while in various places we are told that Jesus Christ is the light, the truth, the life, the way, and the salvation, etc. in every case this is due to his role in reconciling us with the Father. Here we have a paradox, because according to Jesus himself, nobody can even choose to know Jesus to obtain that reconciliation unless the Father first drags him:

> *No one can come to me unless the Father who sent me drags [Greek: helkó] him: and I will raise him up at the last day.*
>
> *(John 6:44)*

No man is dragged where he is already going. Being dragged necessarily opposes natural preference, and is accomplished by the power of somebody stronger. The Father thus drags people to Jesus, and Jesus guarantees that he will save that person on the last day; but then why would anyone be condemned? If the true reason for their denial of Jesus is not that they hated the light, but that they were not dragged by the Father?

This is only one minor example, but it has vexed countless theologians. They study the Word with vigor and dissect the precise language, trying to figure out whether our free will is meaningful in the salvation scheme. Augustine of Hippo, the first true giant of Roman theology, could not make up his mind on it. Almost everyone who ponders the interplay of God and Man reaches the point of giving up eventually, because in some passages we are said to have freedom and paths to choose, and in other places it all seems so fatalistic. Language can drive people mad, especially if they count the words of the Almighty as worthy of obsession. The stakes involved are high, and the Devil is in the details.

IT IS WORSE THAN that. If even the greatest thinkers of history are baffled by God's teachings, having full access to old and better preserved texts, think about the average person. Most people have never had the opportunity to hear God's Word properly. They may lack the Bible in their own language, or access to a personal copy. If the version they receive is somehow corrupted, they won't know any better. It turns out that seeking God does not guarantee you'll end up with reliable texts, or the ability to learn what they're really trying to say. The answers ultimately lie in the books where the details are, not in our positive feelings toward the Almighty.

Some might say that hearing and believing is enough; that a humble faith is sufficient. But is it really that straightforward? Look at what the Apostle Paul warns about in his letter to the people of Corinth:

> *For I feel a divine jealousy for you, since I betrothed you to one husband, to present you as a pure maiden to Christ. But I am afraid that <u>as the serpent deceived Eve by his cunning, your thoughts will be led astray</u> from a sincere and pure devotion to Christ. For if someone comes and proclaims another Jesus than the one we proclaimed, or if you receive a different spirit from the one you received, or if you accept a different gospel from the one you accepted, you put up with it readily enough.*
>
> *(2 Corinthians 11:3-4)*

These people believed too! In their humble faith they were ready to accept whatever they were taught. But they were led astray by cunning, because their faith was too simple.

They accepted what Paul taught, but they also accepted what others taught. So even in the earliest churches there were competing Gospels, and competing versions of Jesus, and competing spirits that are to be shunned and attacked, not tolerated. Being gullible is a real danger, which puts the onus back on the individual to educate themselves about the details of the text. We are not told how subtle these devilish distortions were, but this is a serious charge!

The deceivers are not hypothetical, but part of a larger conspiracy that continues to be a threat to this day:

> *For such men are false apostles, deceitful workmen, disguising themselves as apostles of Christ. And no wonder, for even <u>Satan disguises himself as an angel of light</u>. So it is no surprise if his servants also disguise themselves as servants of righteousness. Their end will correspond to their deeds.*
>
> *(v.13-15)*

Therefore a humble faith is not enough when it fails to protect the truth. There must be spiritual warfare, the armor of God, and the house that can stand when the storm comes, being firmly built on the rock. The Devil and his servants are not idle in the churches, but always seeking to corrupt, often by details.

Who decides?

SO WE MUST ASSESS competing ideas. But the very act of defining "God's Word" is grounds for war. Disagreements about the Bible have led to armies mobilizing, monuments being razed to the ground, leaders being assassinated or exiled, and civilizations overthrown. This is before we get to the question of its precepts and conclusions. Only more division results as we dig deeper into the application of the Word. In such matters, it is dangerous to pick sides, but it is also fatal to remain neutral. And it is evil to be apathetic! It is good to be fervent, but hard to be certain. We are meant to become like little children (Matthew 18:3), but as we will see throughout this part of this book, it takes much more than a childlike understanding to sort out the misconceptions. To be too childlike is to be vulnerable to the deceivers.

Ultimately, all the bloodshed in the world is nothing compared to the fate of the *eternal soul.* Our greater concern should not be peace on earth, but peace with God. When it comes to one's everlasting fate, doctrinal error should produce spiritual terror. Knowledge, on the other hand, should bring serenity even in the face of torture, as it has for countless martyrs. This is the transformative power of God's Word—whatever it may be. In this way, false teachers actually represent a greater danger than armies, since physical weapons can only destroy the body, but deception can erode the foundations of orderly society, and the soul of countless more.

The Devil's mission is to occlude the truth, to scatter the faithful, and to overcome the bastions of understanding by subversion. What better target could there be than the Holy Scriptures themselves? They hold the keys not only to life, but death. With the slightest adjustments in thinking, he can turn the brethren against one another, and turn all of mankind against the proper revelation of God's will. History is full of this. Satan has shown his eagerness to twist everything in knots. And if God Almighty has cosigned this activity by His complacence or His affirmation, how much of this activity can be blamed on Him? Does the fundamentalist have an answer?

EVEN HOLINESS CAN BECOME wickedness in the hands of the untrained, the arrogant, and the self-willed. But is it the skeptic who shows his arrogance by disputing, or the authority figure who presumes to command people about what to think? Even the so-called Church Fathers were often condemned before they were accepted and venerated, and some were called godly until centuries later, when they were deemed to be heretics after all. Traditions, it turns out, are birthed as controversies, and then have to struggle for acceptance. This only shows how meaningless popular objections are in their day; but it does nothing to remove the seriousness of the actual charges. Who is trained? Who is humble? Who is devoted to the truth instead of their reputation?

Paul, in that same letter to the Corinthians in which he warns them not to be seduced by false apostles, pleads with them to recognize his obvious superiority to the proud deceivers, while calling himself a madman and a fool for boasting in the process, because he knows it is unbecoming of a teacher in Christ. His initial humility (in keeping with the modesty of Jesus) became the reason why his pure teachings were taken lightly, and why subsequent liars were respected as greater than him – because the impostors spoke haughtily and charged money, while Paul asked for nothing and seemed like a random fool. Perhaps he should have been boastful from the beginning, and impressed them with credentials and prestige! This is a paradox of Christianity. Today, billions of people are asking what the point of a denomination is. Major traditions still dominate doctrinal teaching and harvest untold sums of money, as if they were a critical part of God's plan. Are such boastful displays of prominence what Paul was trying to accomplish to keep them from listening to false apostles, or have the false apostles won by now, and set up their denominations to capture the gullible by impressive displays?

Status doesn't mean much to a true seeker of wisdom. Such people require arguments, evidence, and study. But when the Bible's verses are broken down into their original languages and definitions are arrived at, interpretations still don't present themselves automatically. They must be triangulated, not arrived at by intuition. We can applaud the attempt to sort out the details ourselves, but the average reader today has little chance. The Devil has already spent millennia spreading his lies, so that sorting out the details feels like looking for a needle in a haystack. Every tradition claims that they are the ones who have recovered and preserved the truth.

To combat the deceit, literacy is important. Unfortunately, reading is a challenge for millions of people. We will deal with the history of the biblical text in subsequent chapters, but for now let's ask if conforming to God's Word is meant to be achieved through a personal study of the Holy Scriptures to begin with. If so, many are hopeless.

It is true, we are told that transformation comes through hearing and believing. A man who hears can only conform to what he has heard from another, but this could be good enough. It would seem to emphasize the communal nature of the church, imitating our best examples and creating disciples. Yet even in an ideal situation, where we have a good teacher with the luxury of covering all of the important fundamentals week after week, the richness of biblical teachings can become overwhelming, because as we have shown already, clear and simple teachings can come together to raise new questions even more difficult than the original problem of ignorance. This is considered a good thing by those who promote tradition as being equal to the text,[5] because they say the exploration of the mysteries of God is meant to be endless and overseen by many overseers, not solved by any given believer in one lifetime. The Church transcends the individual, and the individual is saved by staying within the herd —or, as the case may be, the flock.

Opposing sects agree on this: that trying to conform to the doctrines of the Bible as a lone individual is counter-productive, because we are each too prone to error. Instead, they say we should conform to teachers who have proven themselves in service; namely, men from their organizations. The claim of apostolic succession is sometimes employed to promote an institution as one of few legitimate services. They pass the torch from generation to generation, priding themselves on being old and immovable. Not only is apostolic succession dubious in the

---

5   The Roman Churches (Catholic and Orthodox) hold that tradition is equal to scripture. From Catholic.com: *'In the Protestant view, the whole of Christian truth is found within the Bible's pages. Anything extraneous to the Bible is simply non-authoritative, unnecessary, or wrong. Catholics, on the other hand, recognize that the true "rule of faith"—as expressed in the Bible itself—is Scripture plus apostolic tradition, as manifested in the living teaching authority of the Catholic Church, to which were entrusted the oral teachings of Jesus and the apostles, along with the authority to interpret Scripture correctly.'*

best of cases, but if this is what God requires, it only cuts off more people from His saving knowledge.

Roman Churches say we should practice our faith through sacraments, rituals, and relics, carrying out pilgrimages to holy sites, lighting candles, chanting, and partaking in the busywork of the holy calendar year. This is called liturgy. At the opposite extreme (yet still within the mystical position) are the Gnostics, who believe in an individual revelation of God, but still through various rituals and devotions of their own devising. Meanwhile, progressive modern churches do away with all of it, and say it's as simple as a childlike hope, reaching out and groping in the darkness for contact with God via our broken hearts. No doctrine at all! How can there be such vast discrepancies in God's Kingdom? Is this what the Father intended? If not, why does He allow such monumental blasphemy to go on? The fundamentalist doesn't want to rely on a tradition, but goes to the Scripture as his or her authority. And then they reach the details.

Capturing ideas, or trying to

LANGUAGE BECOMES AN OBSTACLE for anyone who studies God's Word deeply, whether by reading or listening. Especially in the age of the Internet, a believer's optimistic delve into a biblical term can lead to a frustrating maze of wordplay, innuendo, alternative meanings, translation guesswork, cultural baggage, and conflicting traditions. We can't blame the Devil for this, because it is the nature of God's Scripture.

Words are containers for meaning, but the contents are sometimes swapped out over time, or carry different connotations. They take on a life of their own, and we struggle to follow their journey. Etymology and morphology are endlessly rich fields of study on their own, but religious texts can be particularly dense, especially when symbolism gets involved. What exactly was meant in a foreign language 2,000+ years ago is not easy to pinpoint; not that it was necessarily clear to begin with! Even today, when we write, we arrange word-containers in the hopes that our audience shares enough common ground to not get it mixed up. This is made worse by fancy words which sound important, but act more like elastic containers, allowing old meanings to fall out, or new ones to be squeezed in, creating endless misunderstandings. The more loose the language, the more the Devil has room to play.

Religion, due to its tendency to increase in scope over time, eventually provides an all-encompassing and yet unique perspective on things, which calls for coining new words, along with giving old words new implications. They remain containers for meaning, but it gets weird as religious thinkers try to break the limits of what they can comprehend. They try to capture an idea, but sometimes what we're really capturing is nothing more than their own hope of some day explaining something. In other cases, the word is meant to corral a whole herd of scattered ideas that were once roaming wild, just so we don't have to deal with wrangling them individually anymore.[6] In time the conversation changes, and for the sake of tradition, convenience, and organi-

---

6   Terms like the "Rapture", or the "Antichrist" come to mind. These words are used by all sides of an argument as if they refer to a single clear concept, but this hides the fact that, on closer examination, both are hugely speculative, relying on complex assumptions.

zation, we begin to defend words instead of ideas, and ideas instead of truth.

Religion has too many junk words, and unfortunately these are treated as sacred in themselves. Synthetic religious terms are still containers for meaning, but I like to compare them to cages, custom made for the purpose of capturing a rare and mythical idea. We want to trap the idea, even if we've never grasped it ourselves. We might even place a sign on the cage to indicate its contents, so that onlookers will believe that we have trapped the real thing inside. But it's a trick: we haven't captured anything. We just know that there is interest in the subject, or that the idea must exist somewhere, and so we created our own special place for it with a synthetic term, and promote this fancy idea-cage as if we owned what's meant to go inside. If somebody asks for a clear definition, it's like peering into the cage to find the Unicorn. It's never there, but we can stare all day at the elaborate shrubbery of the sophists who have decorated the cage with many interesting compliments, as if to accommodate the Unicorn. We are told not to expect to see it right away, because it may be shy (ie. ineffable) or our eyes may be faulty (ie. we aren't smart enough to understand). When it comes to the Christian religion in particular, the importance of "faith" allows anyone asking too many questions to be silenced as a doubter. Faith is about accepting what you don't understand, after all.

I find that some defenders of the faith glorify religious terms with the acknowledgment that we haven't figured the subject out quite yet, but show confidence that it's only a matter of time before it becomes clear. To continue the analogy, it's like they believe the idea is trapped in the cage somewhere, and it will give up and reveal itself to us eventually. That's not how language or faith works. Fundamentalists have the strongest faiths of all, and this makes them particularly accepting of inter-connected jargon that doesn't really add up.

For all of these reasons and more, the word-cage cannot be questioned. To get rid of the word would let loose the mythical idea, never to be captured again. So we glorify the cage—the terminology—which we are so proud of. Fundamentalists can be very protective of words they know almost nothing about for this very reason. It feels good to speak emphatically about obscure, abstract, and wonderful things. Details diminish this good feeling because they force a person of faith to acknowledge a reason to doubt.

IN ARGUMENTS, POORLY DEFINED terms serve as a natural defense. This makes them popular among cults—or for that matter, any other institution which holds power, and thus benefits by simply existing and remaining inscrutable. Crime organizations, political parties, and lobbying groups alike would love to be shrouded in nonsense. It takes a special kind of organization to embrace transparency and clarity. Most turn the worst gibberish into their central concepts, so that their employ-ees/followers must repeat and dwell on fluff endlessly. Coherent discussion never happens as long as they agree to use the group's magic words. Cult leaders are in no hurry to upgrade flawed terms with more accurate ones, lest the ruse be exposed. If opponents speak out against them by using their words, it's like trying to hammer water. Here, the Devil is invincible, because even the most skilled arguments go in rhetorical circles if they refuse to question the language in play.

Despite the flexibility of loose terms they are not useful for anything meaningful. They become worthless for building larger, more interesting philosophies. Narrowly-defined terms have rigid meanings, and this rigidity is its essential quality, because terms need to have consistent, clear, meaningful relationships with *each other*. A nebulous concept has no proper place in any model, because it fits everywhere and nowhere, and does not support weight when challenged.

Loose language taxes discussions. It always demands context and explanation. This extra context generates more words, which adds to the risk of misunderstanding. And so the cycle goes. Precise language is good, but even a precise term used in a unique religious context tends to become charged by being associated with certain interpretations. For example, we would hope that the word "law" could be an exact, straightforward concept (since we know what is counted as "law" and "not-law" in everyday use,) but in the Judeo-Christian religious context "law" has plenty of baggage. Without doing a deep study of it here, suffice it to say that the Bible contorts the usage of it so badly that it depends entirely on context for meaning by the end, and this has very real implications for doctrines on how to live. Sincere attempts to live "lawfully" according to the Bible have led to radically different lifestyles which not only disagree, but condemn each other. Jesus himself was accused of being a lawbreaker, and toyed with the concept of what is lawful on multiple occasions. Why would God allow this kind of uncertainty when He has all the power necessary to clarify?

We cannot blame the Devil, since he did not write the Bible or put words in Jesus' mouth. We believe God spoke through Jesus and his words are recorded faithfully, yet the true meaning of what Jesus said may be the most debated topic in history. And the details of the language he used is what makes it difficult. For

34

this reason, fundamentalists paradoxically revere what is written in the Bible, and yet avoid looking into too many details.

Of course, we must give examples. These will illustrate how quickly our traditions can be undermined by language.

Note A -   Improper translation choices

BISHOP. (Greek: *episkopos*) Why does the word "bishop" appear at all in English Bible translations (such as the KJV and the ASV)? Was it the most fitting English container to hold the original Greek meaning? Not at all. Most English translations render it more literal, as "overseer". It was rendered as bishop only out of respect for the titles in use at the time of their translation, which had already gone through a long history of association with the Roman Catholicism, and the Anglican Church wished to keep the same general setup.

The etymology comes from the Greek compound term *epi-* ("over") *skopos* ("to observe") being mutilated to the point of losing its beginning and its end, becoming simply "piscop". Then, *piscop* became *bishop* as the hard phonetic sounds were softened.

We know that the term *episkopos* was not designed for Christian churches because it was used in Greek texts that predate Jesus. In the Greek translation of the Old Testament (called the Septuagint, which we will look at later) the exact same term appears plenty of times, where it was used for military captains and overseers of various projects. There were no specific rules or rites implied, nor did it carry the connotation of a lifelong position of divine blessing. If anything, based on the context of the times it is used, the implication would be that such an overseer is a temporary position meant to supervise a specific campaign or project until it was complete.

Churches had overseers even in the earliest days, but not "bishops" in the sense that we think of.[7] Their overseers were tasked with keeping their assemblies orderly and quelling dissent and controversy when people got riled up, which happened frequently. Disagreements in the early church were passionate and required a great deal of reasonable debate. Overseers were respected and serious thinkers, but not fearful figureheads of political power. They were selected by the congregants at times, and sometimes they were seated or unseated by the local governments. Nothing was consistent and systematic in the early church, and so neither was the idea of an overseer's proper role and relationship to other authorities.

Of course the Roman Churches could not have employed the much later English term "bishop" to create their traditions. At first the word did not entail possessing a doctorate in "canon law" and wearing ornate rings, chains, and hats. They used the Latin transliteration (*episcopus*) in keeping with the usage already found in pagan society, which was that of a governing authority. It was not intended to carry a mystical "apostolic succession" idea, but scholars decided later that this idea was correct. In the early church, "bishops" (if we agreed to call them that) were never told to be celibate and remain unmarried, which became a key teaching of the Catholic Church later on. In fact, the Bible clearly teaches (in 1Tim 3:1-7) that a bishop *ought to be faithfully married to one woman* and keep his own children obedient. Therefore, not only is the English word bishop not a good translation to convey the original meaning, but the

---

7   The term bishop came into English use as late as the 1500s, around the time of the Protestant Reformation.

Catholic office of bishop is anti-biblical, and every Catholic bishop would be illegitimate from a biblical standpoint. This includes the "Bishop of Rome"—also known as the Pope.[8]

How have they continued on despite such obvious contradictions? The elastic use of language. Regardless of what they're called, they defend their traditions by saying they are *metaphorically* "married" to the "Church" (which if you recall is the "bride of Christ", and therefore likened to "one woman"—ie. one gigantic, international, all-inclusive church). As for children, again, by stretching the language, they claim that the religious subjects under their rule are like their "children", and therefore, they must be kept obedient! Hence, although their priests and bishops are unmarried, they are still called "father" by their congregations, legitimizing the idea of spiritual parenthood. Of course, this is despite Jesus saying (in Matt 23:9) *"And call no man your father on earth, for you have one Father, who is in heaven."*

CHURCH. (Greek: *ekklésia*) While shocking at first, the word "church" is quite bad at containing the intended meaning. This word ought to be removed and replaced in every English Bible. Etymologically, its various predecessors in Germanic languages are no better. In fact, linguists are forced to guess about how it traveled and morphed so dramatically, so that it has almost no relation to the original Greek word. Whatever led to its English usage, this weird term has inherited all the baggage of Christendom's history. It gives us no clue about what was originally meant by the writers of the Bible.

So what does the Greek term *ekklésia* mean? Here again we have an extremely simple, functional term which long predates

---

8   "Pope" is literally from "papa" in Latin use, meaning "father".

Christianity. It means an assembly. And in the Greek sense, this carried very narrow connotations, which would be useful for us to remember if we wished to honor the intention of the biblical authors. Greek assemblies were not uncommon, but rather central to the core of Greek civilization itself. Greeks established the democratic process, which involved gathering (assembling) the men of a town and letting them air their grievances, suggest solutions, share their ideas, and appoint people to do jobs. They reasoned with each other and cooperated, employing philosophical principles to try to arrive at the most sensible conclusions about what to do. These assemblies had clerks to record their arguments, and overseers (*episkopos*) to make sure opposing sides were being heard fairly. They wanted the assembly's proceedings to remain peaceful and productive. This central tradition, epitomized in the Athenian Assembly (*ekklésia*), is how Greece outpaced other cultures in order to become the greatest social force in history. Needless to say, you would never have guessed all of that in a million years based on the arbitrary English term "church".

Socrates, who is perhaps the most famous philosopher of all time, was famous for going to the Athenian Assembly to make his arguments.[9] And in the Greek translation of the Old Testament we see the word *ekklésia* appearing in places like Deuteronomy 23, where eunuchs and Moabites are forbidden from the "assembly of the Lord". So there was even a somewhat

9   The Encyclopedia Britannica says, regarding the habit of Socrates going to the Assembly: *'Athens was a democracy: all its adult male citizens were members of the Assembly; many of the city's offices were filled by lot (election was regarded as undemocratic, because it effectively pronounced some citizens better qualified than others); and its citizens enjoyed a high degree of freedom to live and speak as they liked, provided that they obeyed the law and did nothing to undermine the democracy and the public good.'*
    (https://www.britannica.com/biography/Socrates/Background-of-the-trial)

generic Israelite meaning, totally unrelated to the later "church" idea. In some English translations it is rendered as "congregation", which is also a sensible choice. Obviously, in the Old Testament, this word had no Greek democracy connotations, but it still referred to that basic, logical, and non-Christian custom which is extremely different from the bloated idea of "church" we have inherited.

We must look at the New Testament itself to see the best proof of all. Turn to the book of Acts and let's read about Paul's venture to Greek cities. Here is a perfect illustration:

> *"...If Demetrius and the craftsmen who are with him have a complaint against anyone, the courts are open, and there are proconsuls. Let them bring charges against one another! But if you seek anything more, it will be settled in <u>the regular assembly</u>. For we truly are in danger of being charged with rioting today, since there is no cause that we can give to justify this disruption." And when he had said these things, he dismissed <u>the assembly</u>.*
>
> *(Acts 19:38-41)*

Interesting! This warning was given by the pagan town clerk who was evidently responsible for creating a record of their chaotic meeting, and who had the ability to dismiss them. Now that we understand their customs a little bit, we can see the oddity in the English translation, which renders the exact same Greek word (*ekklésia*) as "assembly" in this instance, while identical gatherings of Christians magically become "church" by the same translators. Why do they not translate the Greek assembly as "church", or the Christian gatherings "assemblies", if the word is not just similar, but undifferentiated in the source text? Having checked well over a dozen English translations, I found not even one that confused this Greek assembly for a "church", while only a few had "assembly" refer to the gathering of Christians.[10]

We lose nothing of value by being literal and accurate in this case. We instead gain great insight into the simple nature of original Christian practices, influenced by the better part of Greek customs, and we open up the possibility of reform and revival. Perhaps "churches" as we know them should not even exist, and the so-called "liturgy" (also not a biblical term) should be replaced by old-fashioned assemblies for productive discussion, with orderly proceedings, minutes being recorded, and decisions being made, with overseers to moderate. The original Christians were, as the Bible shows clearly, divided into separate assemblies, but not according to denominations, sects, chief personalities, nor doctrinal preferences, but by geography alone, since all of the believers in a city were gathered. They were rebuked when they divided themselves for any other reason. Coexistence was paramount, and forbearing for the sake of the weaker members, and sharing spiritual insights, and edifying by speech and education, using the teachings of Christ and the scriptures as their authority.

We can look at how much evil has been done by the "Church" in its preposterous Roman Catholic form if we need proof of how distorting words by small details can lead to world-altering blasphemies over time.

EASTER. The King James Version adds another example, found with the inclusion of the English word "Easter" in Acts 12:4.

10 They are the Literal Standard Version, World English Bible, Young's
    Literal Translation, Darby Bible Translation, and Worrell New Testament.

Originally, the Greek word here was *pascha*, meaning Passover. This term has nothing to do with Easter, which was a later development in English. The vast majority of English Bibles use the word Passover in that verse because its more accurate, but the old Coverdale Bible (1535), Bishop's Bible (1586), and King James Version (1611) chose not to translate *pascha* but replace it with the name used in their own day to refer to the same calendar event. Thus, they projected a newer concept backward, perhaps not realizing it would create confusion about what would have been celebrated back then.

This particular confusion affected me when I was younger, because, at first, I assumed that Easter must have been established very early on as a Christian holiday, so that even King Herod felt the need to wait to execute Peter until after it was over. That didn't make much sense, however. Why would the same ruler respect a holiday based on the death and resurrection of Jesus Christ, if the plan was to kill his apostles? Then I fell for the common evangelical myth that Easter itself had been around back in the days of Jesus, by that same name, as a pagan holiday honoring Ishtar. But when I checked online I couldn't find any sources for this claim, and instead found that only the English Bibles had this problem.

Easter is not connected to ancient Israelites, Greeks, or Romans. It is in large part a donation of the Germanic king Charlemagne the Great, who conquered the Anglo-Saxon pagans in the name of the Pope around 800 AD, replacing Latin month names with old Germanic ones. Pagan Rome had dominated large parts of Europe centuries before, but Charlemagne represented an entirely different phase of Roman conquest: that of the Catholic Church, as its first Holy Roman Emperor! Ironically, he renamed April—which had been *Aprilis* in Latin—to *Ostarman-*

oth, meaning the month of Ostara. This was a Germanic goddess of springtime and dawn. Her name morphed into *Eostre*, and eventually Easter. The month had been associated with her because it revolved around the spring equinox. The name derives from the same Germanic root where we get "East", because that's the direction the dawn comes from.

So it was among the Anglo-Saxon people, conquered and converted by the Holy Roman Empire, that the Passover holiday was connected to Easter, not because of any allegiance to a goddess, but because it was their name for April. For a month to be named after its most important holiday was not unusual, and *Pascha* meant nothing to the Anglo-Saxons. The Catholic impulse to consume pagan traditions and override them with Christian ones results in all sorts of strange conventions. And while Charlemagne did not intend for his conquered subjects to actually worship the goddess he named the month after, he did want to forge a European sense of unity by reviving their history and imposing a new meaning onto it. The English language would go on to develop slowly, strongly influenced by the Germanic traditions, which in this case meant adopting their word for the holiday. *Pascha* continued to be used by Jews and the rest of the Christian world. For it to end up in English Bibles is purely a leftover of this later development, not a reflection of anything in the New Testament, or its ancient context.

FORNICATION. (Greek: *porneia,* Latin: *fornicatio*) This word appears in many English Bible translations, although others have preferred to say "sexual immorality" to be more generic. Either way, it hardly teaches us anything. To strictly define it as sex between unmarried people is not accurate. The Greek word translates to "prostitution", which is the selling of sex for money.

This financial aspect is important, because its derived from the Greek *pernaō*, which has nothing to do with sex at all, but is a commercial term, meaning "to sell off". Therefore, the selling aspect is what makes it especially derogatory. The Latin *fornicatio* also means prostitution specifically, deriving from the root *fornix*, which meant a brothel where sex was sold for money. Is the Bible trying to warn people not to monetize sex, or to not act like a whore by being so casual about it? Neither of these is what churches traditionally mean by fornication or sexual immorality. To them, it's about the singular act of sex outside of the confines of marriage, period, regardless of intent.

If two young lovers fall in love spontaneously and have sex, and they foolishly believe they will stay together forever, only to be separated by circumstance or parents, have they committed this particular sin? What if they intended to get married, but never could? Neither intended to sell themselves at all, nor to indulge in a carnal fling, but their passionate union was thwarted nevertheless. Love motivated them, not vanity or fun. They may be heartbroken and wish they could reunite. If this is still considered "fornication", then we are saying the sin has less to do with intention and more to do with one's wisdom and preparation. It still does nothing to make "fornication" a good container for its meaning, because it originally implied prostitution. Why condemn misguided lovers who failed to plan their marriage correctly by calling them whores who sell themselves for money? Why not be more clear about what was meant by the authors?

Did the Greeks have a crisis of prostitution? Absolutely, and a particularly Satanic version! Pagan Greeks—before and during the time of the Romans—were notorious for pederasty, or the rape of pubescent boys, for gifts. Their anything-goes hedonism involved pedophilia and bisexuality, and was so widespread and ingrained that it became known simply as "Greek love". This concept became part of Rome's fashion, especially in their upper class.[11] In Rome, sodomy was considered acceptable as long as the older, more noble man was the one penetrating. In Greece, marriage to a woman was seen as the duty to the State, since civilization demanded reproduction, but their sexual temptation was teen boys. One generation of victims became the next generation of abusers, normalizing the cycle.

In one of their more popular traditions, an attractive boy would be abducted from his parents, but only with their permission. The parents knew that the abductor was wealthy or connected. The boy was taken to a special location and seduced by older men with gifts and money (ie. prostitution). Assuming they complied, they would be given prestige later in life and protected as a cherished, idealized symbol of Greek beauty. These boys were called *pornos*; a term we find ten times in the New Testament! But never once does a translation properly convey this history or context with its wording. Just look at this severe warning from Paul:

> *Are you ignorant that the unrighteous will not inherit the kingdom of God? Do not be deceived: neither the sexually immoral, nor idolaters, nor adulterers, nor men who practice homosexuality, ...*
>
> *(1 Corinthians 6:9)*

---

11 Why the church does not expose and discuss this cultural context during the time of the New Testament is a baffling mystery. In Europe, during their Renaissance of Greco-Roman culture, they adopted the term "Greek Love" as a codeword to refer to homoerotic lust without average Christians knowing. See: https://en.wikipedia.org/wiki/Greek_love

Based on this you could never guess that the term translated "sexually immoral" actually refers to a voluntary homosexual whore, but it does. It is the word *pornos*. The ESV, for example, totally omits a specific warning against the dainty, effeminate kind of men who enjoy such things, and lumps this notion together with Paul's warning against those who commit the act of sodomy on another man, as the penetrator. Paul was being powerfully explicit in trying to warn the sexually confused men of Corinth (which was a deeply pagan and Greek city) about their condemnation if they didn't stop their pederasty and homosexual addictions. But the translators always seem to hide these aspects and pretend Paul's words are a generic warning to all men or women who aren't married. Why? Isn't the point of a translation to convey the thoughts of the author, or for that matter, God? And when we know this backstory, other verses become clearer too, which even describe the Greek tradition of kidnapping young men and trying to sodomize them:

> *for [pornos], for sodomites, for kidnappers, for liars, for*
> *perjurers, and if there is any other thing that is opposed to*
> *sound doctrine,*
>
> *(1 Timothy 1:10)*

Paul here makes the direct link for us: between the willing homosexual victim (*pornos*), the abducting abuser (sodomite), and "kidnappers", or more accurately, "men-stealers" as some translate it. The horrible Greek custom was still going on at that time, and many new converts to Christianity did not understand how seriously God condemned it! By making these warnings generic with a word like "fornication" or "sexually immoral" we destroy what is really being said.

Certainly, in the totality of the Bible, God always forbids undisciplined, lustful, flesh-fulfilling, covetous, immoral lifestyles, whether by men or women, homosexual or not. If a person treats sex casually or neglects to overcome their temptations, they are in danger. Homosexual sex is never condoned in any capacity. But the church has, in its long history, dumbed down the Word of God in order to avoid touchy subjects like this. The result is a blanket condemnation of sexuality outside of the technical definition of straight, monogamous marriage, which has long since turned into a legal status by the government and become detached from its essential meaning in the eyes of God. There is plenty of nuance in the Bible, but you would not guess it by the terminology we use. "Fornication" is almost meaningless compared to the variety of specific warnings given in the Greek.

Note B -   Improper non-biblical terms

RAPTURE. (Latin: *rapti*) The word "rapture" does not appear in any English translations.[12] There is also no Greek root word to base it on. It should never have been used as a container for the entire complex study of prophetic events related to the gathering up of the final Christians around a time of tribulation; not even as a way to contain the topic of discussion. Debates about "the rapture" are inane as a result,[13] as they all agree to argue forever about the details of a precise term, but never use a shared definition of the term that comes from the Bible. This supposed shortcut turns into a detour, making discussion worse. It creates a

---

12 Except in its ordinary sense, which means a person being overwhelmed with an emotion. It has nothing to do with divine rescue.

13 By abandoning this term, my own study of the gathering of surviving Christians into the clouds at the return of Jesus benefited greatly.

46

bias in the mind, drawing one's thoughts away from the fullness of the source texts related to the issue and toward the arguments of men, and the history of their disputes related to this bogus word.

TRINITY. (Tri-unity) This is another sacred yet non-biblical term, which to many is the foremost issue of theology. As a container for meaning, it seems to be quite concise and appropriate for what it describes: a threefold unity. The problem is that, while the term itself is very easy to understand, the subject it claims to contain is so profound and ambiguous that the word fails to capture the reality. For those who subscribe to the word, however, this is no matter! They have gone as far as to openly celebrate the paradox as part of the term. To "believe in the Trinity" is to give up on understanding it, by definition. This, like so many other "mysteries" related to the "church", facilitate the Devil's plans more than God's. The interplay of supposed divine authority, physical force, and dogmatic interpretation imbue certain Christian buzzwords with unnatural weight.

By their logic, even the attempt to improve upon the language they use is blasphemy. According to those who revere the Trinity term (I do not say that they revere God, but the Trinity term) there is no possibility of further refinement. The arguments are calcified, their traditions are sacrosanct, and their details are paramount, even when they don't add up. It is the Trinity or death. And I wish this were an exaggeration. There are some respectable Bible teachers who have said publicly that they will "die on this hill" and, being extremely somber about it, added that this was a *literal* promise, meaning they are willing to sacrifice their lives for the term "Trinity" (note: they mean the settled term Trinity, not only an ongoing process of trying to understand the greater concept). For that matter, bishops may be willing to condemn in order to protect "Trinity" as a term. On some level we could consider it one of the greatest marketing campaigns ever, although it does nothing to prove their argument as true. Whether God would approve of such extremism over these details is another question.

Note C -   Literal terms used wrongly

APOSTLE. The Greek word *apostolos* is transliterated into English quite directly, but this doesn't necessarily help. It's used to refer to a messenger who speaks on behalf of another; specifically one sent as an envoy or delegate. The word emphasizes that they are commissioned by some other authority, and do not have that authority on their own. Being an apostle does not inherently denote any power and prestige, because an apostle could be one who simply shares a message for a limited time. Churches have glorified the word beyond reason, probably because they intended to apply it to themselves selectively. Much ado is made about the so-called "apostolic succession" of old churches, who insist on their authority under the rationale that each generation of apostles, since the original twelve followers of Jesus, has theoretically commissioned the next, and therefore ruled out any stray thinkers or leader who might come from outside to challenge them.

At its most extreme, this is linked with Jesus saying (in Matthew 16:9) that he is giving them the "keys of the Kingdom of Heaven" which gives them authority to "bind" things or "loose" things on earth, with the same decision being made in heaven. By claiming that this power is transferable, even modern church authorities can theoretically shape the spiritual world as

48

they see fit. Not much is ever explained in the New Testament about these keys or the rules of binding and loosing, although the twelve apostles (including Paul, not Judas) did make some remarkable judgments as if in the stead of Christ.[14]

The use of the term "apostle" in English translations of the New Testament raises questions, as does the similar term, "disciple". Only two instances are found where the Bible says Jesus made his "disciples" (pupils, students) into "apostles" (envoys) and they are found in Mark 3:14 and Luke 6:13. However, the relevant segment in Mark (ie. "whom he also named apostles") was found to be a later addition by scholars, not in the oldest manuscripts. This opens the possibility that certain men were eager to emphasize their own apostleship as a uniquely powerful role in controlling the churches, and were willing to alter the scriptures to do so. We can't know, but the evidence of two thousand years of history shows how conniving and desperate those who seek power are, bending the text to suit their ambition. It is conspicuous that the term apostle is not used more often in the Gospels, because it would seem to be extremely fitting for the role of Jesus himself. He was sent from the Father as a representative, having authority delegated to him, and tasked with a special mission. The different but related term *apostelló* and its varieties is used many times, such as the demons being *sent out* of the man into the herd of pigs (Mat 8), or the disciples being *sent out* as sheep among wolves (Mat 10). In a very real way, Jesus charged his twelve disciples (pupils) with the same kind of task as he had, and yet the word is mostly

---

14 However, in the book of Revelation, we see Jesus Christ address the assemblies in various towns, and he neglects to take this opportunity to insist on the proper chains of command and succession of celebrity human leaders. He addresses the "angels" appointed to them, making it even more curious how the system of governance really works.

absent in the Gospels. Therefore, seeing as Luke is the one who wrote his own Gospel, as well as the Book of Acts where the term apostle is mostly found, we can see that it was not considered essential to the other writers.

Luke was also a disciple (pupil) of Paul, and Paul himself uses the term apostle in various ways. Usually he is making some other point in the process. He ends up mocking other people who call themselves apostles (2Cor 11:5 and 13) and includes himself as the "last of all" in the group of true apostles, each of whom the Lord appeared to after his resurrection (1Cor 15:8). This suggests that the Greek term, while apt for some uses, was too loaded even back then. It needed to be restricted to the small group of delegates chosen directly by Jesus, confirmed by a special appearance later. And this logic would rule out any succession, even if they did send their own students to places, such as Timothy, since they were not visited by the Lord.

Curiously, the word "disciple" is never used in any of the New Testament letters. It is only in the Gospels and Acts, despite so many people being students of the twelve apostles. How can this be? Again, these words are not essential, as if they hold a special power. Jesus told them to go and make disciples (Matt 28:19) but they stopped using the term fairly quickly. They call each other brothers, and downplay the idea of having their own followers and succession (1Cor 3).

In recent years, an American movement called the New Apostolic Reformation (NAR)[15] has emerged, claiming to have unique power and authority, demanding that others conform to their teachings, using details of scriptural language to justify themselves. The key concept of apostleship is abused by these deceivers, who seek to aggressively dominate matters of policy,

---

15 https://www.gotquestions.org/New-Apostolic-Reformation.html

government, and spiritual warfare in its most literal and mystical sense. They claim to have new prophets, and according to their own statements, seek to control the finances, media, education, and other aspects of American society.

So we see how loaded, poorly-handled terms are used to establish the legitimacy of groups who claim to be the true successors of the twelve disciples of Jesus Christ. But the Bible says the names of the twelve apostles are written on the foundations of the New Jerusalem for all eternity.[16] This means there can never be more apostles who are worthy to be compared to the twelve.

Do we have a succession of bishop-apostles who have been authorized to use the keys of the Kingdom of Heaven, ruling over God's people with supreme authority to bind and loosen the spiritual landscape? Or do we have blasphemous pretenders, who disgrace the scriptures with their schemes and lies, dragging unknown multitudes into Hell after them, as blind men leading the blind? The language allows for both views.

BAPTISM. The Greek word *baptisma* simply means dipping, or temporarily submerging. Similar to the other words we've looked at, this was an everyday Greek term before Christianity adopted it to describe their ceremony. You could accurately say that you baptized your food in sauce before eating it, for instance. The transliteration[17] of the word, unfortunately, fails to convey the simplicity of the meaning, and thus not only allows for various theories on how to baptize, but also opens the oppor-

---

16 *And the wall of the city had twelve foundations, and on them were the twelve names of the twelve apostles of the Lamb.* (Revelation 21:14)

17 Transliteration is different than translation, in that you aren't trying to find an equivalent word in the other language in order to convey the same meaning, but actually spell out or convert the direct pronunciation, so that it can be spoken more easily in the other language.

tunity for a mystification to take place; especially since it seems to be a mandatory ritual with metaphysical potency. People may have reason to fear that getting baptism wrong disqualifies them from its spiritual cleansing power, trapping them in their former sins. And even if this is not technically how it works, the doubt caused by not knowing if your baptism was legitimate in the eyes of God can be enough to weaken one's faith and spoil their sense of having received the forgiveness they sought.

John the Baptist[18] (an expert on baptism's function if ever there was one) said that although he baptized with water for the forgiveness of sins, the Christ would baptize (dip) people with *"the Holy Spirit and with fire"* (Matthew 3:11). We know that the apostles did baptize people in water according to the instructions Jesus gave, and Jesus set an example by getting baptized in water himself. This is fine, but in modern times it's easy to imagine that the word baptism has some magical implication in itself. It has become a way of binding a person's identity, salvation, and faith to a particular church, which is perhaps why churches aren't eager to promote the much more vital "dipping" with the Holy Spirit and fire. But how could they promote such an idea, since they don't look into the interpretation?

If John's dipping into water correlates to what Christ gives us upon our conversion, there's a very odd implication: that we have no basis for believing that the "baptism" of Jesus represents a permanent submersion into either the Holy Spirit or the "fire", whatever that might be. Not only did John not hold people underwater forever (they would have drowned) but the simple meaning of the word baptism itself rules out this idea. Rather, the dipping that the Savior offers is a sample of these things, which nevertheless has a powerful effect on the person. Being

---

18 We could call him John the Dipper if we wanted to.

submerged in water has a cleansing effect on the body, but being submerged in the Holy Spirit might cleanse a soul, or at least give the person a glimpse into the power of God to transform their thoughts and hearts! And since the Holy Spirit is synonymous with prophecy, insights, and spiritual gifts, a temporary demonstration of certain blessings and gifts would also be appropriate. It's a sample of the power Christ has.

Fire is generally a negative experience, but so is being held underwater by somebody else; so negative that it represents being killed, just as the emergence out of the water represents a rebirth. Water is scary, but fire is terrifying. Yet this is good, because it aligns with the feeling we're supposed to have when our hearts stand in front of the Lord: a terrifying conviction of sin, and a heartfelt desire to avoid Hell—which involves the worst flames of all. Therefore, to have a fearful taste of God's judgment is indeed a wake up call, purging our souls. This fire "burns away" the impurities of the former life that need to be discarded. Metals are also temporarily submerged in fire to soften them, so that their deficiencies can be hammered out, and the object can be bent or transformed into the shape desired by the smith. This makes us the work of Jesus. Our spiritual dipping into the fire and Holy Spirit is much more important than the symbolic rebirth of the water baptism. To be all at once purified, purged, weakened, softened, fearful, duly warned, and changed into a new thing despite the rigidity of our stubborn hearts, is a wonderful thing to strive for! But this logic is veiled by the inappropriate adoption of a word that has no native meaning to us, "baptism". A temporary submersion into fire seems very fitting for what Jesus Christ came to do for sinners, and so does a temporary sample of what it is like to be surrounded by the Holy Spirit, which is meant to mark us as a new creature.

If we're on the right track with this interpretation, it is strange why God would allow so much confusion around it. Many denominations (Catholics, Orthodox, Anglicans, Lutherans, Presbyterians, Methodists, and others) baptize infants as standard practice, despite it having no biblical basis whatsoever, and actually contradicting the biblical logic of a sinner being intentionally baptized when they are convicted of sin by God, confessing their need for a Savior. It's true that men's entire households were baptized early on, and that this could involve their children as well. Historians say that the more elaborate ceremony was only developed around the 1300s. Before that, baptism varied, and most who baptized their children thought of it as the Christian equivalent to circumcision, which is wrong.

Infant baptism speaks to how a good thing can lead to blasphemy with a tiny change in details. In an age when infant mortality was high, during the medieval period, unbaptized babies were discriminated against in burials, not being worthy of the "sacred ground" the church set aside for "believers". Babies were not considered Christian unless they were baptized properly by a priest. That an infant was incapable of believing anything about sin or repentance was unimportant to the priesthood, who had the audacity to claim to possess "sacred ground" in the first place. As a cynical scheme for bonding millions to their empire, it was devilishly effective. This is the obvious motive behind such a convenient misinterpretation of what Jesus wanted.

When we remember that baptisms were also performed on royalty and the elite of society – who prized their bloodlines and lineage so highly – we can see how infant baptism served to capture the allegiance of the most powerful people in the world. To induct such important people as early as possible into your organization and surround them their whole lives with the "mysteries" of the "church" and its "apostles" was clever, and it still is. It's no wonder that even the "Protestants" who supposedly broke away from the Roman system kept this essential tool for themselves, growing their membership by targeting inarticulate infants, rather than waiting to evangelize those convicted of their sins.

TONGUES. The spiritual gift of "tongues" is perpetually misunderstood by people, ironically thanks to the choice to render this word literally into a new language, instead of giving the appropriate sense. The ordinary use of the Greek word *glóssa* can refer to a tongue physically, but it was also their word for a certain language. Because ethnicity groups identify themselves by language, it was also used to refer to an ethnicity. A person had a physical tongue, a language, and an ethnicity, and all of these could be referred to with the same word, *glóssa*. The New Testament makes this clear when we see a multitude of diverse people standing before God's throne. Their nations (*ethnos*) and tongues (*glóssa)* are used as connected descriptors for distinguishing the variety of the groups present:

> *After this I looked and saw a multitude too large to count, from every nation and tribe and people and <u>tongue</u>, standing before the throne and before the Lamb.*
>
> *(Revelation 7:9, BSB)*

For the Holy Spirit to give people new *glóssa* had profound implications for Jews and Greeks. It touched on their identity, since language is what separates groups first and foremost. Those who can speak to each other fluently have the potential for harmony. Acceptance, equality, and cooperation can be achieved quickly. God divided mankind into different languages at the Tower of Babel in order to thwart an ungodly project, but the Holy Spirit showed that it was being reversed; God was now using His power to bring together disparate groups through language, for a new project. He wants everyone to be a part of this Kingdom's spiritual construction, regardless of heritage. It has the potential to span the world and unite everyone. Language and ethnicity no longer needed to be barriers. The bigotry of both Greeks and Jews intertwined with having pride in their language, but the Holy Spirit did not force everybody to suddenly speak and understand Hebrew, nor did it cause all of their tongues to speak Greek—God Almighty was showing His impartiality regarding language.

Again, the irony here is that small linguistic choices are exploited to divide Christians constantly, as poorly articulated or translated concepts morph and take on a life of their own in the absence of strong critical thinking. The idea that the "tongues" given by the Holy Spirit are an incoherent babbling finds resonance in 1 Corinthians, but only insofar as Paul warns the men to stop speaking in foreign languages that nobody can understand while in the midst of an assembly that is meant to be orderly and productive! What good is it to speak Mandarin to a group of Greek men if nobody will translate? It would be better to remain silent, Paul says. And yet the confusion around "tongues" has never stopped, and entire denominations have been fueled by demonstrating their holiness through "speaking in tongues" (ie. babbling nonsense at each other) in their "churches". Is it any surprise that these same people often claim the reason for this spiritual elitism is their special "baptism"? Ah, how a confluence of confusion gives all the more opportunity to the Devil, who so often divides and conquers based on details and language!

Who cares about details?

PUBLIC INTEREST IN THE BIBLE is becoming narrower, but deeper. Fewer people believe in the literal aspects of the Bible, but those who are becoming invested in defending it as such are now able to participate in high-level debates in ways that had been impossible for previous generations. Old fundamentalism is disappearing, but a new kind of fundamentalism is beginning to grow; one fostered by search engines, online communities, and fantastic study tools. It is now easy (and free) to cross-check a dozen Bible translations in less than a minute, search specialized encyclopedias, or ask an expert without leaving your home. I personally recommend everyone reading this downloads *e-Sword*, a free Bible study tool, and checks out *BibleHub.com* for quick reference to many different translations, including Interlinear Hebrew and Greek. Faith has always been necessary, but ignorance is becoming optional. The information age has not defeated the church, but shed the untested baggage of the past and transformed it into something leaner and keener. This doesn't automatically mean the Bible is "true", but it does mean that arguments have become stronger on all sides. The bar for dialogue is raised.

Yet still, the Bible remains universally misunderstood. Old-style confidence in the Bible is being hindered as greater nuance takes center stage. We now face a battlefield of propaganda and confusion, as even the basics of the religion are called back into question over and over again. And while answers to these objections are easy to find, they do not agree. Wars of research have migrated from the uppermost royal councils and universities to the streets and slums of social media and home churches.

Regardless of who is correct and who is mistaken about the books of the Bible, such confusion itself poses a problem for us. Logically, in light of an Almighty God, why ought His Word to be surrounded by doubts and disputes all the time? Isn't that a paradox in itself? It is certainly not flattering. Any author whose work is so deeply and uniformly misunderstood must be willing to take some blame for it, right? God had the power to make Himself known by superior means, or through better representatives. The Bible itself could have been developed by an entirely different method if God wanted things to turn out otherwise, and to ignore this controversy is to say that the souls of those who failed to overcome the obstacles of the Bible were not worth the effort on God's part. Or should we blame the devil again, and give him credit for being able to disrupt the plans of the Almighty?

If God's Word is able to heal profound social wounds, enlighten the spiritually blind, and even to save the eternal soul of a person, why then does it so often create social wounds, blind the eyes, condemn the ignorant, and produce chaos? Regardless of whether we read the Bible or find agreement on it, the importance of the Bible in the Cosmic Plan represents a grave threat! Let's be honest: the Bible consists of scattered and fragile documents written by ignorant men in archaic languages, transmitted by painstaking and error-prone methods, collected and preserved by corruptible institutions, translated with an automatic loss of cultural context, and compiled into volumes that defy the average person's reading or understanding. After that, the doctrines were further adjusted not in the book itself, but in the teachings of the churches. Where does that leave us? Does anyone know what the Bible really is? Experts mangle its precepts, the world denies its validity, and even believers neglect to read it. Those who study it struggle to grasp its implications. It is a paradox, especially if God is not the "author of confusion" (1Cor 14:33)!

If the Devil is in the details, does that mean we should avoid details altogether? For some, this is the answer. Whether they end up more or less ignorant than the experts is an interesting question. When you say you "believe the Bible", but you do so without studying it personally, you're basically saying that you affirm its general positive aspects, along with a few of its stories. Is that good enough to be conformed to God's Word, on which our salvation and damnation hinge? If not, the Devil awaits you in the details of the text, where confusion can quickly turn life-giving truth into damnable lies.

FUNDAMENTALISM

WHAT DOES IT MEAN to "believe the Bible"? Does it mean agreeing with its overarching ethics, which tell us not to steal and murder and lie, or does it mean believing its reports of giants as tall as cedar trees (Amos 2:9), and supernatural events in ages before written records existed? Do the stories in the Bible need to be literal and accurate for us to "believe" them, or just profitable to teach from? Is it good enough that they are loosely based on true stories turned into poetic literature? Are we supposed to believe God "inspired" men to write every book in the Bible? And if so, what does that mean? Does God implant exact wording in the writer's mind, or possibly even take control of their writing hand directly, as "ultra-fundamentalists" believe? If God did control the exact wording, then any error would be an indictment of God, and not the fallible men who tried to record the truth. For this reason fundamentalism is a risky stance, because one error can shatter the whole thing.

"Fundamentalism" is counted by scholars to have started as late as the 1920's in America,[19] when a revival movement

19 The Wikipedia page for it says so. As does the Bible scholarship website *The Voice: "Fundamentalism in the 1920s, resulted in the anti-scholarly rhetoric and biases toward biblical study that still echo in the church today."* (http://www.crivoice.org/jedp.html)

rejected progressive scholarship and clung to the old faithful Bible as a self-elucidating work. They taught that it was meant for the average person to read, interpret, and stand up for, without any need for further education. The 1920s dating of fundamentalism is strange. It begs the question of how we should classify English Puritans (1500s), the Dutch Mennonites (also 1500s), or, long before either of them, the French Waldensians (1100s), who counted the Bible as a sacred work intended for the average believer to study personally. Take note that all three of these movements predate the existence of the King James Version Bible, which was only published in 1611, showing how influential earlier translations were on common people.

Each of these movements, including the American one, embraced expert commentaries and wider literacy, but mostly as a supplement to Bible study, but not a prerequisite. Peter Waldo, John Calvin, Menno Simons, and other figureheads may have sparked such movements and given them guidance, but fundamentalism quickly took on a life of its own, turning the Bible—not opinions of experts—into the core of daily church and household authority. Most traditions rely on others to tell them what the scriptures mean, while fundamentalists believe the Bible's true meaning is within reach of a lay preacher, or perhaps even a well-informed congregant. Because of this, many varieties and offshoots have sprung up across America in particular.

There's a good reason why fundamentalism is seen as an American phenomenon. The USA spans a huge geographical area, and has only recently lost the pioneer spirit required to settle it all. Pioneers wanted a land of their own, and their own little church to go with it. Railroads and highways connected these distant towns during the industrial age, while the advent of broadcast media hooked every home and workplace up to mainstream opinions during the transistor age, and this meant places that had once been self-contained and localized were compelled to integrate into the wider society. Now, with the Millennial generation, the Internet has made it impossible to avoid global influence, putting the local leadership in the most difficult position of all. During those years of relative isolation, fundamentalism made perfect sense, because it protected and liberated Christianity from the "authorities" who dominated the biggest churches. They were free from European intellectuals and the Vatican, or for that matter the American coastal elites. America's heartland was defined by home-grown solutions, free speech, and a rejection of worldly power—and naturally, their brand of Christianity reflected that. Major denominations accused these local churches of being born out of schisms, divisions, heresies, and disorder, but that's not true. America's primary philosophy is pragmatism (or at least it was, for three centuries) and fundamentalism became popular because it fixed common problems. It did not start in America, and it is not an American phenomenon, but the two were a match made in heaven—perhaps *literally*.

Freedom in Christ, or chaos?

DISTINCTIONS CAN BE MADE between fundamentalists, especially in regard to which parts of the Bible they emphasize. Unfortunately, the word-container itself has been stretched over time to include any kind of ideological extremist. The term was coined in America in the 1910s to describe those who emphasized five "fundamental" doctrines of Christian theology: (1) the divine inspiration and infallibility of the biblical scriptures; (2) the real virgin birth of Jesus Christ; (3) the unlimited atoning potential of Jesus's death on the cross; (4) the real bodily resurrection of Jesus; (5) the historic reality of the miracles performed by Jesus. A sixth would include the literal return of Christ to earth in the future. Although these may seem like obvious and universal beliefs among Christians, they are not. Liberal theology, for example, has no problem doing away with any of these doctrines while retaining that Christianity is a good story that ought to be analyzed for moral education.

Fundamentalism gained notoriety because it stood against the modern attempt to unite all religions, and instead maintained that those fundamental beliefs gave Christianity exclusive claim to the Truth, the Way, and the eternal Life. They refused to concede that Judaism, Humanism, Buddhism, Hinduism, Islam, or any other religion was a valid path to enlightenment or salvation, because Jesus Christ alone was the Savior and center of the Universe, to whom belongs all worship exclusively. This makes it natural enemies of both ecumenism and Syncretism, which are, respectively: the belief that all *Christian denominations* should unite and reconcile their differences, and the even more extreme position that all *religions* should do the same, because they are all subjective, compatible, and equal.

There was, of course, no gathering of experts to formalize these five (or six) fundamental beliefs, like some modern Council of Nicaea. The term only recognized what was common among thousands of rural churches. These churches were largely Baptist and Presbyterian; both roughly derived from the older Anglo movements of Puritans and Reformed theology. But since the fundamentalists have no official hierarchy or centralized leadership (they rely on hands-on interpretation and self-organization) they are also inconsistent, if not chaotic. They endorse a degree of local and even personal freedom in Christ not enjoyed by Catholic, Orthodox, Lutheran, Anglican, or the more cult-like Protestant denominations, such as Mormons and Jehovah's Witnesses. This liberty allows their style of church to spread quickly, but also makes it impossible to control – which is why, to the thinking of the major organized denominations, fundamentalism is like a weed that grows wildly and saps nourishment from what ought to be a much more healthy, orderly church theology. They are more susceptible to fools, con-men, and false teachers, but also more open to wise, noble, and daring preachers who would never fit into the confines of a big, slow church bureaucracy.

Plenty of Roman Catholics would agree with those five fundamental beliefs, so why are they not included as fundamentalists? Perhaps it's because the label was meant to paint a target on the American Protestant evangelical movement, which rejected the scholar class trying to undermine the rugged old isolationist mentality.[20] The fact that many Protestants embraced this negative term only shows how their rebellious spirit became the locus, or central scene, where fundamentalism grew into a self-aware global force against globalism. It is not a denomination, but a feature that can be found wherever believers insist on elevating the text of the Bible—meaning its historical accuracy, theological claims, and importance to mankind—above all other considerations.

---

20 Let's not forget that American politics underwent the same cultural assault during the early years of the 20th Century. Americans had been isolationist, wanting nothing to do with overseas conflicts, but just as the transatlantic intellectuals found ways to reinvent the identity of America to being the policeman of the world, they wanted Christianity to undergo the same transformation, merging it back into the global community.

Note A -   Outreach and tolerance

A distinction should be made between fundamentalism and the broader, older term of "evangelical", which applies to any Christians who see themselves as messengers of the Gospel, called to proselytize others in their daily life.[21] Given such a gung-ho attitude of recruitment, it may not be surprising that evangelicals are the top religious demographic in America.[22] Fundamentalists are only a fraction of them.

Not every evangelical necessarily believes in those five doctrines, or would allow them to alienate outsiders. For the sake of making the Gospel more appealing to outsiders, evangelicals are sometimes willing to soften and compromise their teachings while talking to strangers. Renowned American preacher Billy Graham was deeply evangelical, but also passionately ecumenical, repeatedly rejecting the idea of proselytizing Catholics, or step on the toes of any denomination, so long as they claimed to believe in Jesus. He was a major player in the "interfaith" scene, trying to harmonize international religious communities. He thought that the job of a Christian was to be an ambassador, a friend-maker, and a reconciler, not a hardline theological bully. He refused to condemn abortion as immoral, supported infant baptism (and did so with his own children), met several times with Popes as his ally, and played loosely with the concept of Heaven for the purpose of winning popularity. He

---

21 This, as opposed to the Catholic and Orthodox methods, which included forced conversions, top-down enforcement, political pressure, and baptizing babies to control beliefs from childhood. They believe their particular Church is empowered to facilitate the Sacraments, which move the believer closer to God with mystical efficacy.

22 *Pew Research Center*, "5 facts about U.S. evangelical Protestants" https://www.pewresearch.org/short-reads/2018/03/01/5-facts-about-u-s-evangelical-protestants/

chastised non-ecumenical Protestants for being exclusionary and harsh.[23] Despite identifying with the Southern Baptist Convention which would normally object to these views, Billy Graham was free to teach such beliefs, without sanction, because there was no central authority to silence him. Extreme evangelism tries to get people in church pews as their top priority, trusting that any confusion will sort itself out over time, while fundamentalists might also call everyone to join their worship service, but warn and reject those who compromise the Bible's authority.

Note B -   War and self-defense

On the question of going to war, there is a long history of disagreement between fundamentalists. More accepted (and therefore less debated) is the question of whether it is justified for a Christian to kill in self-defense. Despite clear instructions by Jesus to treat one's enemies with love and non-retaliation, fundamentalists have been known to give latitude to the individual conscience on this matter too. Baptists are prominent members of the US military,[24] commonly supporting their Constitutional right to own guns and defend themselves and their property, saying that the Bible's prohibition against killing was only about premeditated murder. They tend to lean on the 10 Commandments and Old Testament stories to justify this position, while more radical adherents to New Testament doctrine insist on only pacifism. Look at the Quakers and their

---

23 For more detailed criticism of Billy Graham from a fundamentalist perspective: https://archive.is/XOl2x

24 According to the *Military Leadership Diversity Commission's* Issue Paper #22, a religious survey of military personnel revealed that Catholics were the largest demographic of any religious group, at ~24%, while Baptists were the next highest, at ~16%.

famous "Peace Testimony", which was expressed by George Fox in a letter to King Charles II:

> *"All bloody principles and practices we do utterly deny, with all outward wars, and strife, and fightings with outward weapons, for any end, or under any pretence whatsoever, and this is our testimony to the whole world. That spirit of Christ by which we are guided is not changeable, so as once to command us from a thing as evil and again to move unto it; and we do certainly know, and so testify to the world, that the spirit of Christ, which leads us into all Truth, will never move us to fight and war against any man with outward weapons, neither for the kingdom of Christ, nor for the kingdoms of this world."*

The Amish and Mennonites have been the most explicit of all, with a total rejection of not just war, but self-defense of any kind, or even the protection of their own families,[25] in strict accordance with the example and teachings of Christ and the apostles. A thorough account of their history can be found in a priceless tome called *Martyr's Mirror.*[26]

Somehow, these groups are all passionate defenders of the same book and teachings. Clearly there is something about the Bible that confuses even intelligent and god-fearing men. Are we supposed to incorporate the totality of the Bible's instructions into our worldview and internalize lessons from every story in it, going all the way back to Genesis, or stick with only the latest

---

25 In 2006 a psychotic shooter unleashed random violence on an Amish school group, killing several, and the families immediately forgave him: https://www.theguardian.com/us-news/2016/oct/02/amish-shooting-10-year-anniversary-pennsylvania-the-happening

26 A more full title is *The Bloody Theater, or Martyr's Mirror of the Defenseless Christians.* Written by Thieleman J. van Braught in 1660. Available today via Herald Press. ©1938 Mennonite Publishing House.

set of commandments meant for us? How much weight should we give to the example of Christ himself? He indeed refused to defend himself, but he also evaded capture until his appointed time had come; for that matter, he also owned no property, forsook his earthly family, abandoned his theoretical career in carpentry, remained single and childless his whole life, and recruited many students to follow him around. At some point it seems like we are not meant to emulate his lifestyle, but it also seems logical that these are aspirational qualities. And even if we agree that we are meant to aspire to be like Jesus, why did his own apostles not do so more directly? If it's up to the individual to figure it out, the door is open to any number of wacky interpretations. It's another paradox, calling for people of all dispositions to conform to something both impossible and nebulous.

What's more, we are told to keep and pass on traditions of the church leadership (2 Thess 3:6), but today this could theoretically obligate every believer to listen to whatever harebrained doctrines they inherited from their local pastor. Even more paradoxically, we are told to test and distrust what we're taught (1 Thess 5:21), because the false teachers always lurk in the congregation (1 John 4:1). We are somehow instructed to obey, distrust, test, and enjoy freedom in Christ while being strictly warned to conform and listen to our elders! This is the juxtaposition of the church, embodied in the fundamentalist movement chaos. Justified violence is only one window into this problem.

Note C -   Expectations in life

"Live inspired. Reach your dreams. Become all God created you to be." These are the words that greet viewers on Joel Olsteen's

ministry website, which is loaded with inspirational phrases about God's plans, blessings, and promises for those who follow Him. With 45,000+ attendees at his church every week,[27] and even more followers online and on TV, his sermons have given hope to desperate people in all circumstances. He ranks among other famous charismatic positivity preachers, such as Benny Hinn, Jim Baker, Kenneth Copeland, Paula White, Pat Robertson, and Rick Warren. Without conforming to any denomination, these ministries are often called "Prosperity Gospel" churches. They are primarily focused on motivation, intention, inspiration, and the power of positive or purposeful thinking. None of them would be considered fundamentalists in the traditional sense, because, while they selectively use Bible verses to support their arguments, they are primarily focused on cultivating an environment of positive energy, wealth, happiness, health, abundance, etc. For this reason they are said to be closely connected to the New Thought paranormal movement of the early 20th Century, which was a rival of fundamentalism. The New Thought movement promoted the idea that a person's mentality cosmically altered their circumstances, and that this could be used to magically improve one's life, especially by dwelling on positive hopes and purposeful intention. You can see how this is mixed up with "faith". Aside from being American, there is one major parallel between this movement and fundamentalism, which is that they are all independent, not beholden to any larger hierarchy. As such, they are free to pick and choose which parts of the Bible they emphasize.

Prosperity Gospel teachers often stipulate that people must first "allow" God to bless them, opening up their minds to radical possibilities. They'll also remind their members to give

---

27 Lakewood Church, formerly called the Compaq Center arena. Before being converted into a church it hosted the Houston Rockets.

back to the church, or to others, because charity is one of the keys to keeping the blessings flowing. Therefore, in order to receive the wonderful promises, one must let go of fears and attachments to what they currently own, encouraging people to give away their current savings as donations, to prove that they are ready to handle bigger blessings. Terms like "abundance mindset" are commonly heard. They often conflate Old Testament accounts of miracles with New Testament talk of spiritual blessings, applying the rules of ancient Israel to the believer.

On the other hand, fundamentalists often point to the very example of Christ himself as proof that we should not expect blessings in this lifetime. Christ's sermon on the mount explains that those who suffered persecution, slander, deprivation, hate, etc. would be the ones who got blessed. This stands in contrast to the Prosperity Gospel message. For every promise of deliverance and hope, there is an example of cynicism in the text. Jesus calls the Devil the "ruler of this world"[28] and Revelation shows that he is given power to not only wage war against the saints, but overcome them.[29] We are told: (a) to be sheep among wolves, (b) to be content with food and clothing, (c) to hate our own life, (d) not to love our family members more than Jesus, and (e) to expect to be betrayed by them, as enemies.[30] Such teachings are hardly grounds for happiness. Despite this, we are clearly told not to be afraid.

Consider the paradox of fundamentalist Christian expectations over the centuries, even if we don't include today's wilderness of scam artists. There have been long stretches of prosperity and

---

28 John 12:31, 14:30, 16:11. He also says his kingdom is "not of this world" in John 18:36.
29 Revelation 13:7. See also Daniel 7:21 + 25.
30 (a) Matthew 10:16. (b) 1 Timothy 6:8. (c) John 12:25. (d) Matthew 10:37. (e) Matthew 10:36.

peace for certain groups of Christians, while others have been ravaged by war, persecution, and evil. Did the oppressed Christians fail to have an abundance mindset, or did the Devil afflict them because they were righteous? And if they were afflicted by the Devil, isn't that supposed to be a blessing, not a curse? Should we pray for riches and ease, or should we focus so much on the afterlife that we abandon any notion of material comfort here on earth? If the rich man cannot enter Heaven, why would any Christian want to be rich? Wealth allows us to solve problems, give charitably, create jobs, care for our families, and do good in the world! Is that so evil?

> *But if anyone does not provide for his own people, and especially those of his household, he has denied the faith and is worse than an unbeliever.*
>
> *(1 Timothy 5:8)*

Is the ideal Christian meant to live as impoverished evangelist, ready to be betrayed by their family, leaving their household, roaming the world, and ministering to others by surviving on donations and volunteering, or should they stay put, be wise, create value where they are responsibly, and prosper so that they can take care of their community, donate to others, and become a boon to the needy? Both have a case to make.

Note D -   Holy Hebrew

How far can fundamentalism's devotion to the text go? Some say that because God "does not change" (Malachi 3:6, James 1:17) He would also not allow His Word (ie. the holy scriptures) to be "changed" either. Therefore, they indulge the idea that God must have spoken Hebrew when He created the Universe, for example. Since He doesn't change He must never have spoken anything other than Hebrew, nor ever will. Adam and Eve spoke Hebrew, being taught it from God; and so did Noah before and after the world was flooded; Hebrew was spoken during the building of the Tower of Babel, when all the people were unified with one tongue. And then, when God confounded the languages of mankind, Abram and his home tribe of the Chaldeans were not affected by the shakeup, so they kept using it. Naturally, by this logic, Abraham's descendants faithfully maintained this tongue throughout Egyptian captivity for centuries until Moses arrived, who wrote perfect Hebrew without any change in syntax or style from Adam and Eve. This gives us a direct, lossless record of holy words from the beginning of Creation to the writing of the Torah.

Of course, fundamentalists believe Moses wrote the first five books of the Bible by divine inspiration, and that his version is exactly what we ended up with today. From Genesis to Deuteronomy, every word is considered a divine choice. This means any deviation from the original text, including translations, would defy God's nature, because it would prove that He does change after all. Normally, they'll also insist that the King James Bible was the perfect translation of this perfect Hebrew, and therefore we can have confidence that no words, meaning, or context were lost over the millennia.

Evidence to the contrary is easy to find, and we will show it in the subsequent chapters. Those who believe in the unchanging holy Hebrew language are trying to honor God and the Bible, but they inadvertently humiliate themselves and reject the reality of the Scriptures. Those who study the real history of

Hebrew may have less cognitive dissonance, but paradoxically a less glorious claim about God's consistency and ability.

Note E -   Hidden Torah Codes

IN 1958, A RABBI named Michael Weissmandel found amazing patterns in the text of the Hebrew Old Testament. To him, they suggested that the original authors had encrypted secret messages in the text which had to be deciphered using mathematical codebreaking techniques. On the heels of World War II, codebreaking was a prized skill across the world, and many intelligent people began to wonder whether there might be codes hidden in older, mystical, and important texts as well. Shakespeare and other classic writings were inspected, but the Bible was the real prize.

Rabbi Weissmandel's "Bible Code" pointed to a miraculous set of codes in the Old Testament, which he was eager to share. These, he said, had to be unchanged over the millennia, belonging to the original Hebrew text. They were also beyond what any human could have accomplished. Weissmandel called his method "equidistant letter sequences" (ELS) because they spelled out a word if you started with a certain letter and then searched for the next letter in the word only after skipping a certain number in between, with the next in the sequence being *equally distant* from the previous ones. For example, the Hebrew word **Torah** (or TORH, because it has four letters in Hebrew, or תּוֹרָה) was discovered repeating in both Genesis and Exodus in perfectly equidistant sequences, repeatedly, with its letters separated by 49 letters each time! Meaning, if you started by picking the first instance of the "T", and then 49 letters were skipped, the 50th letter would be an "O", and then another 49 letters, followed by the "R", and then "H"; and then, even more amazingly, another "T" would be found after another 49 letters, and the cycle would repeat! The number 49 is significant to Jews because it is the square of seven—the holy number. The number 50 is also important because, according to the Torah, every 50 years is the Israelite Jubilee. Weissmandel's discovery has been excitedly shared with Jewish and Christian believers ever since.

This is almost impossible to believe, suggesting it must be a miracle. This remarkable sequence begins immediately, starting with the last letter of the *very first word* of Genesis (Hebrew: *bereshit*, or בְּרֵאשִׁית), and supposedly repeats throughout the entire book of Genesis! And, it is then found repeating again in the next book, Exodus – and again starting with the very first occurrence of the Hebrew letter ת. This makes it statistically impossible for it to be a coincidence. Likewise, the Hebrew word for TORH spelled backwards (HROT) is found in both Numbers and Deuteronomy, the *last* two books of the Torah. Would you believe that these are also separated by the magic number 49, in equidistant letter sequences? That's the claim of the Hebrew codebreakers. Fundamentalists can't help but rejoice when they hear about such a breakthrough discovery, proving that the Bible is a work of God's inspiration.

Why would the last two books of the Torah spell "Torah" backwards, while the first two spell it forward, and what about the middle book, which they both "point to" – Leviticus? Here, the Bible Code says, we don't find any ELS for the word "Torah" one way or another. Instead we find a different code. This time, in Leviticus, it's an ELS code for the name of God, **YHWH**, repeated every seven letters! Yes, they say that you can find Y-H-W-H in a repeating sequence every seven letters throughout the entire book of Leviticus. Combined with the ELS codes for

Genesis, Exodus, Numbers, and Deuteronomy, what else can we do but praise God for demonstrating His glory this way, woven secretly into the first five books of the Hebrew Bible?

Jewish and Christian teachers alike love to promote the discovery of secret codes hidden within the Hebrew Old Testament, which supposedly show the divine inspiration of the books.[31] With advent of computers, the ability to find patterns has sped up the process. Ambitious new discoveries have been made, like finding not just one word repeating, but *groups of words* related to each other, in sequence. Computerized codebreaking for Bible secrets was pioneered by Dr. Eliyahu Rips, who is a staunch Jewish Rabbi. As a fan of the ELS codes pioneered by Rabbi Weissmandel, he wanted to go even further, showing how the entire Old Testament was written by God down to the letter. What he found surprised him, and he has been writing about it ever since. He even makes videos about it in his old age.[32]

Skepticism about such claims is an instant invitation to be judged by fundamentalists, since a belief in the supernatural quality of the Bible is automatic to them, and therefore anyone who promotes God's Word as a miraculous work is presumed to be on His side. It would almost be weird if there weren't mind-blowing discoveries happening regarding the Bible with the advent of every new technology, and if Jewish scholars were not leading the way! As His chosen people, they are gifted greater insight and appreciation of the Hebrew than anyone, and there-

---

31 As per the Christian apologetics website *Different Spirit* (https://www.differentspirit.org/evidence/torah-code.php) *"The discovery of significant words spelled out at equidistant skip sequences of letters in the original text of the Hebrew Bible is powerful evidence that the Bible is a work of God rather than a work of men."*

32 *The Bible Code 100% proven scientifically - Professor Eliyahu Rips* https://www.youtube.com/watch?v=2v6Ej78TwZU

fore they are closer to the divine tongue which upholds the Universe.

Going further yet, some fundamentalists who believe Dr. Rips say that he has proved that God planned all major world events from the beginning, and encoded them into Scripture to be discovered thousands of years later by advanced codebreakers. Some of his codes require a little bit of imagination, but they do seem incredible once they are discovered and pointed out. For example, a blatant reference to the English playwright Shakespeare emerges using the ELS computer method, Dr. Rips says, because it finds these words in the original Hebrew: "MacBeth", "Hamlet", and "stage". How else would this have appeared in the text as a code, except by divine providence? Another one refers to man landing on the Moon, with the words "spaceship" and "Apollo 13" found in equidistant letters. A very important event, at least for modern Zionist Jews, is the assassination of Yitzhak Rabin, the fifth prime minister of Israel, and this also has a prophetic code found in the Bible: "assassin", "Amir", and "Tel Aviv". Of course America is included too, with the death of John F. Kennedy Jr. being alluded to with the sequence "to die" and "Dallas". Are these starting to sound like a stretch? The author of *The Bible Code* book (published 1997), Michael Drosnin, says there are thousands of related word groups revealed in the Hebrew like these, and he considers them all valid proof of God's authorship of the Hebrew text. He would like you to buy his books to find out more, so you can show them off to your friends and family.

In the next chapter we will look at arguments against the ELS discoveries and their promoters, including an anti-Christian bias that is sure to raise the eyebrows of fundamentalists.

Faith and fault

AS WE PROBE DEEPER into the problems of the Bible and its proponents, I ask the reader to stay highly aware of their discomfort level. Ask yourself how it affects your judgment: do you want to jump to conclusions to escape doubt? Do you latch onto convenient explanations because you are losing your footing? If we believe in something as fantastical as miracles, do we quickly lose our hope because of something as trivial as wording differences? Does the cosmos really depend on the Masoretic Text, or has God tolerated imperfections in His Word?

Faith is indeed empowering, and fundamentalists more than anyone treasure the Bible as a weapon for spiritual warfare, but does this weapon lose its edge when we find mistakes? On this point, I wonder if Jesus did not give us a reminder about having the correct priorities in times of uncertainty:

In the fourth watch Jesus approached them, walking on the sea. And when the disciples saw him walking on the sea, they were alarmed, saying, "It is a spirit." And they cried out in fear. But immediately Jesus spoke to them, saying, "Be glad, it is I; do not be afraid."

Then Peter answered him and said, "Lord, if that is you, invite me to come to you on the water." And he said, "Come." And when Peter was lowered out of the ship, he walked on the water, going to Jesus. But when he saw how the wind roared, he was afraid; and, beginning to sink, he cried out, saying, "Lord, save me." And immediately Jesus stretched out his hand, and caught him, and said to him, "O you of little faith, why did you doubt?" And when they entered into the ship, the wind ceased.

Perhaps this happened as a lesson to all future Christians. We defy rational limits by maintaining fundamentalism, but sink into the waters of doubt as soon as we use our rational mind and acknowledge textual problems. If this is the lesson, we truly must stand on what seems to be water. But before we make up our mind either way, we might ask whether a fundamentalist ought to have faith in the *purity of the Bible* itself as a flawless and unified document, or rather a faith in the *God of the Bible*, despite whatever difficulties we encounter.

DOUBLE-EDGED SWORD

GOD'S WORD IS APPROPRIATELY described as a "double-edged sword", because it is bound to cut both ways. Interpreting the Bible's stories as a collection of genuine historic accounts told with divine precision—as the fundamentalists do—means that the books must be defended as an all-or-nothing package of holy revelation. Any error or inconsistency would invalidate the entire fundamentalist position, sending them into a tailspin of doubt, desperation, and fear; hardly appropriate for people of faith. On the other hand, as soon as we recognize embellishment and human error in the text, we must concede that many biblical "facts" could be inaccurate. And if the stories are not accurate, how can their morality remain true?

Perhaps the most controversial story in the Bible is Noah's Flood, in which God decides to destroy all (land-based) life on the planet. We are not told how many humans were killed in this event, but the figure could easily be in the billions, if the circumstances described are accurate. Genesis clearly describes humans of the pre-flood era as being virile and healthy for hundreds of years longer than today, meaning that a single man could have fathered thousands of children in his lifetime, if he kept multiple wives simultaneously; and we have no reason to assume they wouldn't, since God did not restrict it by any intervention, but instead told them to multiply and subdue the earth.[33] This is not to mention the death of animal life, which would have been immeasurable. To most people familiar with the story, this account is understood to either be an ancient fairy tale, probably meant to trick kids into believing one thing or another about God and mankind's weird relationship, or an inadvertent admission that the God of the Bible – and therefore any religion which honors Him – is evil. Collective punishment is not a Christian principle, after all, and there is no bigger collective judgment than Noah's Flood. It is almost a good thing that few believe the story is real, because it would entail a serious debate about the fairness of God. However, as I pointed out in the introduction to this book, Judgment Day handles this controversy.

Christians of the non-fundamentalist variety have defended Noah's Flood *as fiction,* saying that, while God did not really kill mankind and all those animals in a global catastrophe, the story remains an important lesson about how God has a limited tolerance for evil, and will some day judge the world again. But how does this make any sense if it's not accurate? There is no lesson if it's not true. Either mankind wasn't particularly evil in ancient times—in which case God had no reason to threaten them with judgment in the first place—or there really was an epidemic of corruption so extreme that they deserved to die, but yet God was unwilling to do it. Instead, these defenders think God created an empty myth about an extinction event that never happened, perhaps to fool His people into thinking that's the kind of deity He was.

---

33 Even if God had forbade polygamy or casual sex, people were obviously rebellious and did whatever was right in their own eyes.

If Noah's Flood is a myth it means there is no basis for thinking that God will judge mankind in the future. If the story is true it almost certainly guarantees that God killed millions of children whom we would consider innocent, rather than eliminating the worst people in a more surgical operation, and educating those who could be taught to do better. If it's fiction, then the Israelite authors could have made up any number of additional details to frame God's judgment in a better light. If the story is a sincere attempt to record some tribal history, which recollects a smaller but still authentic event, then the blunt and fragmentary nature of the flood narrative suddenly makes more sense, but begs the question of what kind of nuance is missing from the original story, or how much was added to it as it passed from generation to generation, and from subculture to subculture. It would be more like a rumor about some distant civilization's tragic collapse than a meaningful explanation of how God's people emerged from prehistoric times. All of this speculation is unpleasant, but considering the magnitude of the implications one way or another, it's necessary to weigh the possibilities.

Some say the story is an allegory for the Bronze Age Collapse, which most historians believe explains archaeological evidence found across the Mediterranean. They have found many indications of great civilizations meeting a sudden ruinous period around 1200 BC. The later roles of Assyria, Egypt, Greece, Babylon, and other major powers were supposedly defined by this sudden onslaught of drought, war, pestilence, and so on. If the Bronze Age Collapse allegory theory is true, then the particulars of the biblical account would still be "false" in the fundamentalist's eyes, because they didn't really happen the way the Bible describes. Yet in the eyes of scholars, the accuracy doesn't matter. The story becomes valuable and illuminating because they value an interpretation from ancient poets trying to make sense of their world. Which of these sides has more evidence, and what would it take to disprove either one? In the next book we will deal with the paradoxes of scholarship, so don't assume they have all the answers. Scholars are great at presenting problems, but they don't like to be put under the microscope themselves.

Did ancient Israelites even believe their stories were literal, or did they know they were creating fables meant to comment on the Bronze Age Collapse? Hebrew scholars who indulge the fundamentalist perspective recognize a much deeper commentary interwoven throughout Genesis about fallen angels, giants, demons, and miracles surrounding the rise and fall of great nations, but this is laughed at by any mainstream scholars. If the flood narrative is accurate, its simplicity could be imply that whatever is mentioned is only a small reminder given to people who would not have needed to be taught about the global deluge which shaped their world. Rather, the interesting part for them would be a reminder that the same Almighty God had a part in shaping all the other major world events from the beginning, and how it ultimately ended up with an emphasis on Hebrew slaves in Egypt.

Genesis doesn't make any particular apologies for God's ethics, nor does the Old Testament praise Israel as perfect. Judgment Day is never spoken of, meaning there is no recourse to that logic. So if the stories are tribal propaganda, they are surprisingly critical of themselves. "Like it or not," they seem to say, "this is our God, and this is how things ended up so bad." To those who can't get over such tall tales it is only an embarrassing reminder of how ignorant people once struggled to grasp the natural order. This is where the details matter again, and the sword of God's Word threatens to cut the one who wields it too arrogantly.

THE "DISCOVERY" OF "BIBLE CODES" is another example of how fundamentalism enables radical ways of thinking, but ends up backfiring under examination. Skeptics have a lot to say about the equidistant letter sequences, and although they are hardly vital to a fundamentalist faith, there are always theories like this coming and going to inflate the confidence of the congregation. Add up the total number of false prophecies, hoaxes, and fallacies spread throughout their churches and you have a rather embarrassing legacy of ignorance. And while a Christian may brush aside this legacy as irrelevant, as it does nothing to hinder their own personal faith, each failure to acknowledge and hold accountable the deceivers sends a message to the rest of the world about Christianity. It tells the world that our faith is all equally disingenuous fluff, untested, clinging to anything that gives hope, even delusion, without standards, happy to exploit childlike hopes and fears and make money in the process.

Just look at how ELS itself becomes a double-edged sword when you use it as proof of divine inspiration. For as impressive as it sounds at first, skeptics have looked up their own sequences to challenge the fundamentalist's certainty, finding phrases like "There is no God" occurring five times in the Hebrew Torah, as well as "God is dead". Why would God plant these messages in His Word? If one code is valid, why not another? We shouldn't be cherry-picking which patterns are meaningful and which aren't based on what we personally want to be true. We must take the codes at face value and let the evidence lead us.

Michael Drosnin popularized the ELS discoveries with a book called *The Bible Code*. He's the one who began to apply the findings to future predictions around the world. However, even Dr. Rips himself disavowed the work of Michael Drosnin:

> *I do not support Mr. Drosnin's work on the Codes, nor the conclusions he derives....All attempts to extract messages from Torah codes, or to make predictions based on them, are futile and are of no value. This is not only my own opinion, but the opinion of every scientist who has been involved in serious Codes research.*[34]

Skeptics say that they've found ELS codes just as impressive in classic tomes like Herman Melville's *Moby Dick* and Leo Tolstoy's *War & Peace*. Of course, due to the emphasis on Hebrew as the divine script, these studies were carried out on Hebrew translations of these works, not English. They supposedly found "predictions" of the assassination of not only Kennedy, but Lincoln, Yitzhak Rabin, and Princess Diana. This may be one reason why Dr. Rips wanted to distance himself from Drosnin's excessive methodology and prefers to stick with his own techniques.

Watching Dr. Rips explain his theories, it becomes immediately obvious that his emphasis is less on the Torah itself, but on validating a specific Hebrew version of the Torah alongside the rabbinic commentary on it, called the Talmud. This is disheartening news for Christians, because the Talmud is a strictly counter-Christian work, created centuries after Christ, promoting the ongoing necessity of the rabbis and their traditions, and thus invalidating the notion of anything having changed due to

---

34 For this quote and more arguments against the Bible Codes, see *The Skeptic's Dictionary* page for it, archived here: https://archive.is/RFEtO

Jesus Christ, the new covenant, or the church. Dr. Rips finds innumerable proofs that the "Rashbi" (their equivalent to Jesus, in terms of foundational teaching) provided the keys to understanding the Bible Code. He employs weirdly specific references to Rashbi's commentary in seemingly coincidental places, highlighting how certain words (when using Rashbi's commentary as a key) intersect on the visible page, vertically and horizontally, since Hebrew lettering is laid out on a grid. In other words, the Bible Codes presented by Dr. Rips are not compatible with Christianity, but Rabbinic Judaism.

A more expert analysis than I could give was carried out by Jeffrey H. Tigay of the University of Pennsylvania in a paper titled *The Bible "Codes": A Textual Perspective*.[35] I will only quote a small portion of his essay here, to show how quickly the claims of the Bible Code revolve around rabbis and the Talmud, not the Old Testament we might normally think of:

There are three types of such arguments.

(1) The simplest is to find words of related significance in close proximity to each other. For example, in Exodus 11:9-12:13 (see Fig. 1), the Hebrew title of <u>Maimonides' Code</u> -- <u>Mishneh Torah</u> -- is found by starting with the M in Moshe in 11:9 and counting every fiftieth letter until the word "Mishneh" (M$NH) is spelled out, and then starting with the second T in 12:11 and counting every 50th letter three times until "Torah" (TVRH) is spelled out. Between the first letter of Mishneh and the first letter of Torah there is a gap of 613 letters, equal to the traditional number of the Torah's commandments, which <u>the Mishneh Torah explicates</u>.

---

35   https://www.sas.upenn.edu/~jtigay/codetext.html

Maimonides (full name Moshe ben Maimon/Rambam) is one of the most influential rabbis ever, the author of *Mishneh Torah,* which was compiled around 1170 AD, well into the Middle Ages. It is a dense work of legal and doctrinal instruction, telling Jews in Europe how to obey God and satisfy the law. Needless to say it is totally divorced from Christianity. It was intended to condense and interpret the Talmud for regular Jews who were struggling to keep their religion in the face of Roman Catholic pressures and persecutions. The notion that the Torah gave Israel 613 commandments is an interpretation of Maimonides that gets adopted and repeated by Christians ignorantly. Yet fundamentalists have picked out certain nice-sounding details of all such analysis and celebrated them as proof of the Bible's inspiration. A double-edged sword indeed.[36]

BUT EVEN IF THIS Talmudic focus weren't the case, there is a bigger problem: there is no such thing as one definitive Hebrew text of the Old Testament. Researchers must select a version of the Hebrew, and the ELS codes all vanish when another version is selected.

> *Our oldest and best Hebrew manuscripts, the Aleppo Codex, the Leningrad Codex (basis of Biblia Hebraica), the Cairo Pentateuch and the Damascus Pentateuch Codex all differ in their letter sequences because of spelling variations which throws off the ELS.*

---

36 Jeffery Tigay says: *Finally, the most sophisticated and computer-dependent of all are such phenomena as the "famous sages" experiment, whose proponents -- Prof. Eliyahu Rips of the Hebrew University Mathematics Department, along with Doron Witztum and Yoav Rosenberg -- argue that one can find ELS-coded references to the names of several dozen <u>medieval rabbinical sages</u> and, nearby, in statistically improbable proximity, their dates (Hebrew month and day) of birth and/or death.*

(https://www.bibleandscience.com/bible/codes.htm)

We will discuss the nature of manuscripts and Hebrew at length later in this book, but for now it is enough to realize that the Bible Codes are putting an extreme emphasis on certain versions that suit them, while ignoring the ones that don't. Fundamentalists like to imagine that there is one standard and universally-accepted Hebrew basis for the Old Testament, but it just isn't that simple. Even the precious "Masoretic Text" is not uniform, but has variations that make it impossible to say which one is the true and faithful version.

Details matter when we're talking about divine precision. In the video by Dr. Rips I mentioned earlier, he and his defenders try to discredit the findings of skeptics by saying that they all falsified their results, and did not use the true spellings and conventions that were provided by the Rashbi. So much emphasis is placed on the uniqueness and improbability of these odd occurrences that a lay viewer is forced to either trust the rabbinic experts and marvel at the math, or suspect them of playing fast and loose with their facts, telling the audience what they want to hear, knowing that all but the most diehard skeptics won't bother to verify their claims. Those who do will be easily smeared because of how much work they put into discrediting something that seems to praise God!

CONFUSION IS A MASSIVE problem in Christianity today, but you might not notice unless you wade into the swamp of discourse in social media. I speak from observation, having spent thousands of hours in the Christian side of TikTok over the course of three years. Currently TikTok remains the most popular social media app in the world, with billions of minutes of content on almost every conceivable subject. There, I amassed more than 215,000 followers over the course of a year, explaining my views on Revelation and common misconceptions about the Bible, gaining millions of likes on my videos and an enthusiastic base of users asking me questions. To traditional Bible teachers I represented exactly the kind of out-of-control speculation they were fighting against, but to many others I represented clarity around some of the most difficult subject matters. Needless to say, in such a position I had a constant influx of everyday concerns from Christian men and women. At the same time, I was locked into the algorithm of Christian theories and interpretations, along with people's favorite clips of sermons, educational videos, and scholarly analysis. It was a crash course on the state of Christian thought today.

What I saw was a hurricane of half-truths, blending tidbits of scholarship with a reverence for church traditions, mixed with popular assumptions and a sprinkling of personal bias. People were certainly finding answers to their questions, but for every question there were three conflicting alternatives, leaving the end no better than the beginning. New findings collide with old traditions, and critical examination upends simplicity. Harmony was nowhere to be found, and people ended up picking their favorite creators to champion, trying to send them against each other in doctrinal duels. As Facebook and other social media giants were dying, thousands of obscure discussions were migrating with them, providing all the proof I needed that this was not endemic to TikTok alone, but a worldwide free-for-all.

Does God want such confusion? And if there is no end to the disputes, is it better to remain ignorant and faithful than becoming knowledgeable but uncertain? This is a question for fundamentalists and scholars alike, because it's not clear who pleases God more.

The good old fashioned church system may seem like a good solution to the mayhem, but it became clear to me that many of the Christians online were reaching out specifically because their good old fashioned church did not have answers. We can think of the rise of online educators as a symptom of the failures of the local church. People who love the Bible are not satisfied with bland assurances when they know there is an exciting world of discussion one click away.

Harmless contradictions

A SIMPLE EXAMPLE MAY test the fundamentalist's certainty, and show whether they are willing to receive or dismiss the evidence. We will look at one book of the Bible which twice comments on the grandchildren of King Saul, which seems to have a contradiction in it. It's a harmless thing, with no theological weight, but because fundamentalists want to believe that every detail of the Hebrew text is divinely perfect, even this will threaten to destroy their assertion.

In 2 Samuel 6:23 (KJV) it says, *"Therefore **Michal the daughter of Saul** had no child unto the day of her death."* This is a very straightforward statement. But in the same book, in 21:8 we read about the same woman: *"...and the five sons of **Michal the daughter of Saul**...."* Obviously this means she did not remain childless until her death! Keep in mind that these are not two different books, but both 2 Samuel. So which verse is correct?

We can't know. The KJV retains "Michal" in both instances, but other English translations avoid this contradiction by placing the name "Merab" (another daughter of Saul) in the second instance. What gives these other translations the gall to change a name in the Bible, and why does the KJV seem to have a mistake?

For its translation of the Old Testament, the KJV relies on what are called the **Masoretic Hebrew Text** manuscripts. In their ignorance, fundamentalists often consider these to be a perfect transmission of the pristine words given to Moses himself by God directly. The KJV translators faithfully reproduced the error they found in the Masoretic Text because they dared not question what was holy. Furthermore, they were instructed to use another popular English Bible as their guide:

> _For the Old Testament, the Masoretic Hebrew text was used_, and for the Apocrypha, the Greek Septuagint text was used primarily…. Since the translators were instructed to use the Bishops' Bible (1568) as a guide, which was a revision of the Great Bible (1539), which was a revision of the Matthew's Bible (1537), which was a revision of Coverdale's first Bible that included all of Tyndale's translation work (1535), the King James version includes much of the wording of the Tyndale and Coverdale translations. Thus the preface to the first edition says that _the translators never set out to make a totally new translation, but to make out of many good ones, one principal good one._
>
> (Cedarville University digital commons, KJV section "The Texts")

But it gets a little more complicated than that. Scholars are aware that the "Masoretic Text" is not a singular thing. They instead call the efforts of the Masoretes[37] a "transmission circle" that had at least eight different editions. There's the famous Leningrad Manuscript, Jerusalem Manuscript, Koren, and Hilleli Manuscript. (Incidentally, the Bible Code researchers such as Dr. Rips, for instance, only use the Koren edition of the Masoretic Text, apparently because their discoveries aren't replicated in the other editions.) All of these editions are considered excellent copies of the same books, but even they have variations which are undeniable, because the preservation of the Masoretic notations point them out to us.

> *The expression "transmission circle of the Masoretic text" attempts to define those manuscripts demonstrating an unmistakable similarity to the likeness of the version arising from the thousands of Masoretic comments, <u>which were formed to preserve the semblance of a specific version selected as an authorized text, the one known as the "Masoretic Text"</u>. Even within the "transmission circle (Maagal Hamesira) of the Masoretic text" <u>there were variations between well-known exemplary texts,</u>*
>
> *(Prof. Menachem Cohen, Department of Bible Studies, Bar-Ilan University, Faculty of Jewish Studies, 1997)[38]*

Scholars point to lesser known manuscripts as being correct in this instance, because they don't have a contradiction about

---

37 Groups of Jewish scribes tasked with developing a system of markings and page organizations to help standardize the Old Testament Hebrew's proper pronunciation and grammar. Hebrew does not have proper vowels and spaces, so it becomes a nightmare to read without these helpful markings. Their work began in the 5th Century and continued until the 10th Century. There were several different Masorete groups who produced many variations between them.

38 This letter preserved here: https://archive.is/PxosB

Michal's childlessness in them. These other Hebrew manuscripts did not have a well-funded community of scribes working to preserve them like the Masoretic editions, so they are fragmented and don't have a full copy anywhere. All Masoretic Text editions, however, do replicate the same contradiction about Michal as far as I know, which is why English translations based on it reproduce the same error!

Extreme fundamentalists must grapple with the dilemma: how can the Masoretic Text simultaneously contain a contradiction, and yet be the perfect transmission of God's Word? It may seem irrelevant to us, but to them it would be the end of the world—literally! The most extreme Christian fundamentalist proponents of the Hebrew text's importance cite a passage which says that Jesus is *"upholding all things by the word of his power"* (Hebrews 1:3, KJV) to mean that the very language of the Hebrew Scriptures upholds Creation! They argue that Jesus in some sense produced the Old Testament autographs[39] personally, because he is the living Word of God since before the world was formed, in accordance with the Gospel of John. And this is also why *"Heaven and earth shall pass away, but my words shall not pass away."* (Matt 24:35) Yes, the cosmos itself depends on the Hebrew Bible being 100% accurate and perfectly preserved, and what's more, the King James Version (they think) is a perfect translation of the perfect Masoretic Text into English. That's a

---

39 An "autograph" is the original work in its entirety, not a copy. A "manuscript" can be a copy of an autograph, but unless it is somehow marked it is impossible to know whether an old manuscript is the original or not. It's very rare for an original autograph manuscript to survive for centuries, making it necessary to rely on whatever the oldest available manuscripts are. These old copies are seldom fully intact either, forcing scholars to piece together fragments. The more copies there are, even if they're fragmented, the more scholars can compare sections to see if there are variations between them, and try to weigh the evidence of what was probably in the original.

92

lot of pressure to put on a book, but it's what makes fundamentalists so excited to be part of it.

Upon realizing the error of the Masoretic Text, it may be tempting to reject entirely their Hebrew manuscripts, using only the Greek Septuagint, for instance. Fundamentalism insists on inerrancy, after all. But where are the perfect manuscripts? Some are non-contradictory in the instance of Michal and her children, but they are not perfect in other instances. Can we judge which manuscripts are perfect anyway? Are we forced to choose which ones seem the least incorrect? Most Christians who say they love the Bible still don't know anything about manuscripts or the differences between them. The point here is not to lecture you on manuscripts, but to ask what an intellectually honest fundamentalist should do with tricky questions of errors, inconsistencies, and logical oddities. Did God inspire perfect books for all future generations to reproduce exactly, or have we inherited a jumble of imperfect stories?

As somebody who grew up in a fundamentalist tradition, I have been astonished at the existence of any errors, and found myself quickly searching for an explanation to whisk it away. The tiresome, complex, academic field of study around this or that language or manuscript is not what I signed up for when I said that I "believe the Bible". But I can see why many are led into that path. What concerns me is that a genuine love for the Bible can so easily end up at a point of anxiety and uncertainty. The more we look into the details, the more we discover a world of educated opinion[40] over controversial problems, rather than religious certainty. And although the example I chose was delib-

---

40 If you find yourself hating these educated opinions, you should look forward to my next book in this series.

erately not important, I have to wonder why God would allow this kind of confusion to seep into His Word.

There are many examples of textual inconsistency and narrative variations in the Bible and its manuscripts, as the same story is retold in different books, or even different parts of the same book. Fundamentalist preachers can make a whole career of defending the Bible with clever explanations, but the logic can become so strained that it no longer feels like we're winning, but just coping with a problem. And that itself is unnerving for a faith that is meant to be established by the Almighty God of the Universe, who is "not the author of confusion".

> *For God is not the author of confusion, but of peace, as in all churches of the saints.*
>
> (1 Corinthians 14:33, KJV)

QOHELETH, WHO ARE YOU?

THESE WORDS SPOKE DEEPLY to me the very first time I read them as a child:

> *"Vanity of vanities," says the Preacher. "Vanity of vanities! Everything is vanity."*
>
> *(Ecclesiastes 1:2)*

I finally encountered someone who broke through the noise of ordinary chatter and grieved for the world openly, with the appropriate level of sorrow. Clearly, whoever wrote the book was occupied with the tragedy of mankind's existence, which I saw as the most blatant controversy ignored by everyone. As I read further, the passage connected this lament to the mystery of time and nature in a way that even a child like me could understand:

> *"What does a man profit from all the work for which he toils under the sun? A generation goes, and a generation comes, but the earth remains forever. The sun rises, and the sun goes down, and hurries to the place where it rises. The wind blows to the south and goes around to the north; around and around goes the*

wind, and on its circuits the wind returns. All streams run into the sea, but the sea is never full; to the place where the streams flow, there they will flow again.

"All things are full of weariness. A man cannot utter it. The eye is not satisfied with seeing, nor the ear filled with hearing. What has been is what will be, and what has been done is what will be done, and there is nothing new under the sun. Is there a thing about which it can be said, "See, this is new"? It has already been in the ages before us. There is no memory of former things, nor will there be any memory of later things, yet to exist among those who follow after."

(Ecclesiastes 1:3-11)

The sensation I felt was excitement and relief, because for the first time in my adolescence I knew that I was not crazy. Here, in the beloved book found everywhere, was the proof! Not only was it available and beloved, but regarded as God's own Holy Words, perfect in its messages, and designed to teach crucial wisdom, meaning nobody could dispute it! It was unlimited ammunition to make my case if I needed to.

Before Ecclesiastes, I gravitated to things like dark comedy and cynical media, because they at least pointed out the weary nature of life and acknowledged its absurdities. I had no concept of what philosophy was, nor did I have access to classic litera-ture, so I took what I could get in pop culture. When somebody in school mentioned that the ancient Greek philosopher Socrates had been the greatest thinker ever, I quickly sought his teach-ings in the school library. Plato's dialogues, which were designed to recall and simulate what it was like to talk with Socrates, lit the fire of philosophy in me. Although not as profound as the book of Ecclesiastes, which I would discover later, Socrates clearly cared more about truth than reputation, politeness, or circumstance.

Already, around the age of 10, I had noticed that circumstances were always changing, so that there was no point in talking much about anything. Only truths—I would later learn they were called "principles"—remained forever, and these could apply to many circumstances. Why wasn't everyone focused on the eternal, since the temporal was all vanity? Just thinking about how Socrates, who existed thousands of years before I was born, remained relevant and powerful ages later proved me right: circumstances could change a million times, but principles were pristine and stable. Things that were important were actually timeless. Yet, as Socrates himself acknowledged, this awareness of the transcendent made daily life all the more tedious, and he knew better than anyone that he did not possess the Truth.

After Socrates I started to read philosophy more habitually, but found myself disappointed in all the wordy intellectualism they devolved into. It was like they were trying to turn life into math and solve the equation, not speak from the heart about what it meant to be alive. I tried to digest the Proverbs of the Bible next, but while many of them were precious nuggets of advice, they lacked structure or elaboration, and so they couldn't capture the full conundrum. That is when I stumbled across Ecclesiastes. It was strange to find a book in the middle of the Bible that I had never heard preached or referred to, despite going to Sunday School my whole childhood and attending plenty of church services besides. As soon as I read it, I knew it was far greater than Socrates. It was so profound that to me, Ecclesiastes was for years the only book of the Bible that I knew for certain was not a man's opinion, but God's Word.

IF THE WORDS I loved were written by King Solomon, which is what both Jewish and Christian traditions hold, then they carry a special significance in the history of the world. That's because King Solomon was granted divine wisdom beyond what any ruler had obtained in the past, or would ever obtain in the future (1 Kings 3:12)! That last part is very important, because it tells us that nobody else will ever surpass it. Such writings would transcend all circumstances and be invaluable for every generation. I loved to know that God not only blessed Israel with such a king, but that this king in turn produced wisdom that can instruct mankind thousands of years later. Even if his message is uncomfortable, that would be precisely the point: a wise man ought to force the world to face uncomfortable truths. Truth is disruptive, and that's good.

But there is a problem. Scholars doubt whether Ecclesiastes was actually written by Solomon. In fact, the vast majority are now certain that it wasn't him. In the *Lexham Bible Dictionary*, for example, Solomon's authorship is presented as only one of several traditions about how the text came to be. They acknowledge that the opening words point to Solomon as the author (as the author identifies himself as "the son of David, king in Jerusalem") but Britannica comments on this point:

> *Though these words can only refer to Solomon (fl. mid-10th century BC), the frequency of <u>Aramaic forms</u> and the book's <u>rationalistic contents</u> date it sometime about <u>the second half of the 3rd century BC</u>.*[41]

---

41 https://www.britannica.com/topic/Ecclesiastes-Old-Testament

This is blasphemy to a fundamentalist. It means that the book itself is lying to us, because it was not really written by David's son, or a king of Israel. It means it was written less than 300 years before Jesus, during the inglorious days of the Second Temple, instead of 900 years earlier in the glory days of the united kingdom.

We can ignore the arguments of scholars easily, if we have nothing invested in the text. If we won't be using it for anything anyway, who cares? But if we are trying to preach, teach, or derive important insights from it, this controversy changes everything. For even one book of the Bible to be a hoax means that the entirety is no longer God's Word, for one. Everything is suddenly up for grabs.

Even if nobody else cares, it matters a great deal to me personally whether it was created by a random plagiarist or by King David's blessed son. This book is a treasure to me. It shows how a wise ruler regards the endless toil of life, and even comments on God's role in orchestrating it:

> *I, the Preacher, was king over Israel in Jerusalem. I determined in my mind to search the wisdom of all that is done under the sun. What an immense weight God has laid upon mankind to occupy them!*
>
> *(Ecclesiastes 1:12-13)*

If Ecclesiastes is a forgery, or a "pseudepigrapha" as scholars call it when somebody fraudulently attributes their writing to a different person, then it is no better than trash. It wasn't written by a man with special wisdom from God. Not only would it be deeply fallible, but even wrong and harmful. It wouldn't belong in the Bible! God could have had a completely different message he wanted people to hear, and Ecclesiastes turns it all upside down and makes grand statements that are folly!

And indeed, there are those who say it never deserved a place in it to begin with. The Jewish Encyclopedia states: *"The canonicity of the book was, however, long doubtful ... and was one of the matters on which the school of Shammai took a more stringent view than the school of Hillel;"*[42] meaning that even early rabbis disputed whether it should be included in their standardized holy texts. *"Endeavors were made to render it apocryphal on the ground of its not being inspired ... or of its internal contradictions ... or of a tendency which it displayed toward heresy—that is, Epicureanism"* a worldview named after the Greek philosopher Epicurus, who lived from 341-270 BC.

Imported wisdom

EPICURUS, LIKE SO MANY Greek thinkers, was influenced by Aristotle, who sought to explain the composition of the universe from a rational perspective. In a sense, he started the process of turning philosophy into math. He lived three hundred years prior to Epicurus, and was a successor of Plato (who himself was a successor of Socrates). Epicurus was active during the period known as Hellenism, the infusion of Greek thinking into Jewish culture. Epicureanism emphasized a materialist worldview, because, as Aristotle observed, the universe was a giant system of interlocking physics that perpetuated each other in cycles,

---

42   The controversy of the rabbinic schools of Shammai and Hillel will be reserved for a future book. The link to this entry can be found here: https://www.jewishencyclopedia.com/articles/5415-ecclesiastes-book-of

with or without human involvement. As such, Epicurus was also a rational hedonist, because materialism meant everything was ultimately pointless, and so the best somebody could do was try to enjoy life and minimize trouble. Seasons followed seasons, generations followed generations, and everything had natural deterministic cycles. Such a philosophy rendered both ambition and superstition foolish. The best kind of pleasure, he said, was tranquility and friendship, because kindness was reciprocated with kindness, and brotherly love with brotherly love. Unlike the author of Ecclesiastes, however, he taught that there must not be any gods, or if there were, they were totally unconcerned with humanity, and therefore mankind should have no fear of them, nor of death. His teachings were popular, and were spread around as a "gospel" – that is, a message of good news.

> *So my heart began to despair over all the labor I had toiled at under the sun. When a man exists who has labored with wisdom, knowledge, and skill, and he must give his legacy to a man who has not worked for it, this too is vanity and a great evil. For what does a man profit for all the toil and striving with which he labors under the sun? Indeed, all his days are filled with grief, and his task is sorrowful; even at night, his mind does not rest. This too is vanity.*
>
> *Nothing is better than for a man to eat and drink, and enjoy his work. I have also seen that this is from the hand of God. For without Him who can eat, and who can find enjoyment? To the man who is pleasing in His sight, He gives wisdom and knowledge and joy, but to the sinner He assigns the task of gathering and accumulating that which he will hand over to one who pleases God. This too is vanity and a grasping of air.*

When I think of King Solomon writing these words in his old age my thoughts resonate with them deeply, but the moment I consider that they could be a forgery by some anonymous writer in the Second Temple period, I become disgusted at their presumptuousness. This exposes within me a dichotomy: I can just as easily despise any part of the Bible if it were shown to be false, but as long as I have confidence in its veracity I cherish it. What I considered the greatest wisdom in the world can instantly become galling and provocative nonsense when I think of it as inspired merely by the philosophy of other thinkers, not the moving of the Holy Spirit. It is not good enough to treat it as a masterful Jewish work of literature inspired by Hellenistic imported ideas. With Ecclesiastes in particular, the vanity of vanities would be too ironic. "My God, why did you not supplement this book with better proof of its authorship?" I want to ask. "If it wasn't written by Solomon, why did you allow it to enter the canon of the Bible and reach my childhood eyes?"

There should be no doubt that Epicurus' teachings ended up in Israel, because once you understand Hellenism it becomes unavoidable; we will talk more about that later. The question is whether Ecclesiastes was written later than or prior to Epicurus. If it was written later, it would make sense for a Jewish scribe to adapt it, because Jews respected the great thinkers of their day and wanted to have an equivalent in their own society. Attributing their writings to Solomon retroactively is well within the Second Temple tradition, because scribes and Jewish thinkers produced countless pieces of literature and claimed they were from all sorts of historic figures. If that sounds surprising, keep in mind that Jews were occupied by foreign powers, and governed by various innovative pagan empires for centuries at a time when God ceased to speak to them or help them with miracles and prophets. They were relatively unimportant all throughout the Second Temple period. Israel's envy of heathen kingdoms is a common theme throughout the Old Testament, as God Himself compared their impulses to whores who lust after stronger nations, rather than trusting Him.

Debating about the origin of Ecclesiastes by looking at its philosophy in English translations will not yield much insight, however. There are always differences and similarities of ideas, and we can't know who said anything first. Scholars go to the oldest Hebrew manuscripts for more technical clues, and the results are not good. As we've already noted, there are plenty of Aramaic loanwords mixed into the Hebrew text of Ecclesiastes, which wouldn't make sense before the Babylonian captivity, since the Aramaic-speaking Persians only conquered Israel and imposed their language on them after Babylon demolished Solomon's Temple – and this was long after Solomon died.

What's in a name?

THE BOOK OF ECCLESIASTES also does not mention Solomon by name at all, but rather, it claims to be "the words of **Qoheleth**, the son of David, king in Jerusalem". You won't find that word in your English version, however. In Hebrew, Qoheleth is a term related to a person who assembles others, or collects things,[43]

43 It might help to know that the very name "Ecclesiastes" is based on a
    translation of this name Qoheleth into Greek. You'll recall that the Greek
    term *ekklésia* means "assembly"; when the Hebrew was translated into
    Greek, they named this book after its supposed author, who identified

although there's no usage of the term outside this book. This person's name is translated as "Preacher" or "Teacher" in English translations because of this role as a gatherer of men.

Scholars point out that everybody who descends from David's lineage has a tendency to call themselves "the son of David" as a way of glorifying themselves. Supposedly, ancient Jews called themselves somebody's son in an attempt to identify with their legacy and attributes. This is why being "sons of God" is a valid expression despite not being literally true, or Abraham being the father of countless people long after he died.

To contrast this Qoheleth pen name, we see that in the book of Proverbs it states explicitly that they are *"The proverbs of Solomon, son of David, king of Israel."* Why would Solomon give his name in one book and not another? Ecclesiastes could be considered his greatest work, and he should be proud of it, shouldn't he? It's true that this Qoheleth character says that he was king over Israel in Jerusalem (1:12) and that he was wiser than any of his predecessors (1:16), which should leave only Solomon, but this means little to scholars. They point out that later authors loved to attribute their work to famous old figures so they would feel more weighty. The Book(s) of Enoch is a classic example. And, while it isn't likely based on the evidence, there could also have been a king who came after Solomon who considered himself a "son of David", who genuinely believed that he was wiser than all of his predecessors, and who decided to call himself Qoheleth in a book. Whatever the truth is, this matter of names already puts my favorite book of the Bible in very murky waters.

---

himself as an assembler. English Bibles adopted the Greek title verbatim (as they did with books such as "Genesis", "Exodus", and "Deuteronomy", rather than translating them into English counterparts.)

Timing is everything

NOW THE STRONGER OBJECTION. Yale Bible Study puts it bluntly:[44] *"The language of the book shows that it cannot have been written in the age of Solomon. This is Late Biblical Hebrew, heavily influenced by Aramaic, and with many points of affinity with the later Hebrew of the Mishnah [Talmudic books created hundreds of years after Jesus]."* Not only is the writing style reminiscent of the Aramaic which would be introduced to Israel much later, but there are also a small number of direct loanwords. Between these two factors, scholars believe Ecclesiastes was written late as 200 BC, when the Greeks ruled Israel but an Aramaic-infused version of Hebrew was common. How troublesome for our philosopher-king!

> *The Hebrew in which the present form of the book is written represents a very late stage in the development of the language. The text contains loanwords from Persian and Aramaic and uses certain vocabulary and grammatical forms that only became common shortly before the beginning of the Christian era. Thus the present form of the book must come from the Second Temple period at the earliest (i.e., from at least four centuries later than Solomon), and Qoheleth is probably a wisdom teacher who takes on the persona of Solomon in order to argue that even someone as wise and as rich as Solomon would say what the Teacher says, if given a chance to do so.[45]*

---

44 https://yalebiblestudy.org/courses/wisdom-literature/lessons/ecclesiastes-study-guide/

45 Kathleen Farmer, "Ecclesiastes, Book of," ed. David Noel Freedman, Allen C. Myers, and Astrid B. Beck, *Eerdmans Dictionary of the Bible* (Grand Rapids, MI: W.B. Eerdmans, 2000), 367.

Is it possible that this celebrated book of the Bible, which was the inspiration of my love for it in the first place, was a hoax?

INSPIRATION

HOW DO WE DEAL with this? If you're like my younger self, you believe that Scriptures are holy, and therefore incorruptible. It's as if they have divine protection. Furthermore, even if there were a possibility of error, Jews would have treated it as too sacred to change, and thus never allowed it to be altered. I liked to imagine that they had an impeccable, miraculous transmission of God's Word all the way from Moses to Jesus, and from Jesus to us today. That was a nice thought. Certain things are out of the question when you believe this. Translations don't really make sense because *divine precision* would be the whole point. Somehow, I still believed the English Old Testament was safe from corruption—perhaps by miracle as well. I gave no credit to the hard-working intellectuals who have slaved over tiny discrepancies in old manuscripts and tried their best to convey it. As any translator knows, it's impossible to keep the literal meaning of a text and still do justice to the deeper meaning it's trying to communicate. If you don't accept this, remember that this is why the Tower of Babel incident—with confusion of the languages—was so effective at separating mankind into unique nations that could no longer cooperate together.

Do we believe translators are also inspired by God, just as Moses was when he wrote the Torah? Scripture does not say that much, but we often do. This presumption should not be forced to carry the weight of the whole Bible.

If you've never studied the topic of old manuscripts and the difficulty of keeping accurate copies, it can be easy to assume the "Tanakh" (the Hebrew term for the entire Old Testament) was directly sent from God, like the 10 Commandments given to Moses on Sinai. Perhaps you think they were written by God's own finger. For some readers this assumption is so strong that it becomes a tenet of their faith, and so they would defend such a fallacy even after correction. Believers across the denominational spectrum misunderstand the Bible's origins or avoid thinking about the problem of language. They think that "the Hebrew Scriptures" (by which they imagine some singular, perfect version) are not only sacred in the human sense of being invaluable or connected with religious revelation, but flawless words from God Himself.

Such people always cite 2 Peter and 2 Timothy as proof that the biblical writings are divinely inspired:

> *knowing this firstly, that no prophecy of scripture is of private interpretation. For no prophecy ever emerged by the will of man: but men spoke from God, being moved by the Holy Spirit.*
>
> *(2 Peter 1:20-21)*

This seems to settle the matter right away. But if you look carefully at the passage (yes, at those pesky details) you will notice that it does not actually say what most people think it does. Here it is again with the ignored parts emphasized:

108

> *knowing this firstly, that no <u>prophecy</u> of scripture is of private interpretation. For no <u>prophecy</u> ever emerged by the will of man: but men <u>spoke</u> from God, being moved by the Holy Spirit.*

As you can see for yourself, it only speaks of *prophecies*, and says nothing about all the other things in the Bible, such as: (1) historic figures and their deeds; (2) genealogical lists; (3) law codes or commandments; (4) speeches given by people; (5) wisdom poetry; or (6) the connecting stories between these things. That leaves out the majority of the Old Testament! And doesn't even touch on whether the New Testament writings should be included. We don't know what Peter considered the "scriptures" to be exactly. We can make educated guesses and assume he went along with the general consensus of the small Jewish-Christian world, but does this make sense? Jews had disagreements even back then about what was inspired, and Christians were rebellious against many traditions.

Ecclesiastes is an example of a book with a disputed status before Jesus was born, so I wonder, did Peter consider it scripture and/or prophecy?

Jews had also lost texts along the way, and certain books were not respected as much as others. Would Peter include the questionable Book of Enoch, or other books we consider non-inspired? The canon of the Tanakh was generally in place by the time of Jesus, but as we continue to examine the Bible's story we will realize that Peter himself could not have known which versions of which texts perfectly transmitted their original meaning, and which were errant. And even if he somehow did know these things, he did not care to share that knowledge with us, leaving us to make assumptions.

Peter says that prophets spoke—*not wrote!*—as the Holy Spirit moved them. This may be significant. Prophets personally wrote their prophecies down sometimes, but sometimes they spoke while relying on others to remember and record them correctly. Other times, prophecies were given in private, such as in dreams, in a situation where no writing would be possible. These were not even spoken, but only revealed and recorded later. Whatever the case, let's assume that all the followers of the prophets did record their speeches perfectly, and nothing was lost between the time it was given by God to the writing of the account. Even here, we must wonder if these accurate records were preserved and transmitted perfectly during subsequent generations. After all, there are examples of small but meaningful differences in various manuscripts when it comes to prophecies, too. Not all of them can be correct simultaneously, but they are all "holy scripture".

Recall that the "Late Hebrew" of Peter's day was distinctly different from Classical Hebrew that the servants of the prophets would have recorded in originally. Isn't that a change, of sorts? Our own struggle to recover the richness of archaic languages shows us that we can only make educated guesses. By the time of Peter, were the hand-copied manuscripts recording the prophecies of Samuel or Elijah still accurate? And if they were, can we trust that they still are two millennia later?

Looking at Peter's day, we find that the majority of things written by Holy Spirit filled believers were rejected or lost by the church. This means not everything written by Christians were considered inspired either. They picked only a few things to publish and maintain copies of. Did Peter know which of these texts were going to be worthy to be counted as new holy scriptures, and which were not? Was he even trying to reference new writings? This is why we can't use his statement to validate every New Testament claim – especially since, as already stated, it only applies to prophecies.

Amazingly, the New Testament even mentions instances of ordinary believers speaking prophecies to their peers, and yet it does not record their words! Paul goes as far as to tell those in Corinth, *"Pursue love, and earnestly desire the spiritual gifts, <u>especially that you may prophesy</u>"* (1 Cor 14:1). He continues by telling them prophecy is superior to other spiritual gifts because it builds up the church and helps people (v.3-5), and that doing so convicts visitors in their hearts, causing them to believe and worship God (v.24-25). And yet, where are their prophecies recorded for us? Either the hope of Paul never came to pass, or they neglected to preserve these prophecies in writing. We get the sense that the Holy Spirit was pouring out plenty of prophecy in those days, and yet we have very little evidence of what was said.

Therefore, not every prophecy was recorded, and if they were, they became lost in time. This is stunning to us today, when it seems that prophecy has ceased and we would love to witness such a blessing. But they, even when they knew God was speaking through them, did not transmit it for future generations. And what does this tell us about the nature of early church record-keeping? Are we missing vital prophetic writings that put the truth in a new light? We have only a few letters, but there was an exciting wealth of knowledge being poured out in that day.

And again, since Peter limited his statement to only prophetic records, this would leave out most of the New Testament, which is largely made up of remembered historic accounts and teachings about doctrines. These would fall *outside the guarantee* of divine authority, and could be "of private interpretation" or exist "by the will of man", couldn't they?

Look at the Gospel of Luke, which begins this way:

> *<u>Since many have attempted to compose a narrative</u> about the matters which have taken place among us, just as those who were eyewitnesses from the beginning and ministers of the word delivered by them toward us, <u>it seemed good to me</u> also, <u>having researched</u> accurately all things from the start, to write to you in an orderly fashion, most distinguished Theophilus, so that you may know the certainty of the things in which you were instructed.*
>
> *(Luke 1:1-4)*

Does Luke claim that he has received a sudden and amazing revelation from God, whether in a vision, or by the Holy Spirit weighing heavily upon him and compelling him to write the account verbatim? No. He only says that it "seemed good" to him, and that he "researched accurately" on the reports of "eyewitnesses" (who may not have a perfect understanding) for the sake of this Theophilus character. Luke introduces himself as a journalist, in other words, doing research. He is not speaking with the absolute certainty of God's Word, nor a divine inspiration at all. Why would he not admit that the Holy Spirit was granting him miraculous knowledge if that's what happened?

Should we ignore these facts and falsely stretch Peter's assurances to include everything in the Bible? Are we doing the Bible justice by twisting it out of proportion to suit our comforts? Should we put words in the mouth of Peter to promote a nice sounding lie? I don't think so. Here again, in plain view of the fundamentalist, one of their favorite teachings is debunked as soon as we pay attention to the details.

LET'S NOW LOOK AT THE OTHER famous passage about the Bible's divine authority and accuracy:

> *But evil people and charlatans will progress from bad to worse, deceiving others and being deceived. You, however, must continue in the things you've learned and become confident in. You know who taught you, and how from infancy you have known the holy writings, which are able to give you wisdom for salvation through faith in Christ Jesus. All scripture is inspired by God and practical for instruction, for conviction, for correction, and for training in righteousness, so that the person dedicated to God may become competent and equipped for every good work.*
>
> *(2 Timothy 3:13-17)*

This is a favorite passage among fundamentalists. When we look at the details, what does it say, and what does it mean?

Before looking at the portion dealing with holy writings, let's acknowledge that it begins by warning about *increasing deception*. So unless this prophecy was untrue (which would be ironic), we know that many will be deceived as things "go from bad to worse". Two millennia later, this deception should have grown enormously! Knowing the Devil's goals, this means deception about the Bible as well.

Now as for the matter of holy writings, we can see that Paul was telling Timothy to have confidence in the writings he was trained in. But we don't know which versions of which holy writings Timothy was instructed in exactly, or which traditions were pure and untainted. It only takes a little yeast to spread through an entire loaf (Galatians 5:9). The difference between a holy text and a corrupted, yeast-infused one could be tiny. Nobody wrote down and preserved Timothy's studies, so we run into the same issues as with Peter, and must jump to the same kind of assumptions. Paul also does not define what he (or God) considers to have been "breathed out" or inspired by God.

This passage also does not mention whether these writings—no matter how inspired they originally were—have always been transmitted faithfully, or if they always will be going forward. Peter limited his remark to prophecies, but Paul is making a broader statement about "all scripture". Which ones, and which variation of each? Presumably he means only the Hebrew texts, and not those produced by the Egyptians, Babylonians, Persians, Greeks or Romans, or the new literature created by the Christians. But we just don't know.

A BIGGER CONCERN MAY be that Paul characterizes these scriptures as being practical or *profitable*, but does not say they are *accurate historical records*. Technically, one cannot use 2 Timothy 3 to argue that distant historic events and conversations between biblical figures are accurate. He says they are practical, specifically *"for instruction, for conviction, for correction, and for training in righteousness"* in order to produce good works and keep faith in Jesus. That's a big difference in terms of usage! After all, even fiction can be profitable for training in righteousness if it inspires people and teaches them lessons they need to learn; just look at parables.

114

You could argue that God would never allow errors if He is the one inspiring, but this immediately raises the question of what "inspiration" even means. Paul invented the word used in the Greek here (*theopneustos*) and it is not clear whether it means God filled the writer with the Holy Spirit (since "spirit" is always associated with breath) to the point where they could speak/write infallibly, or if they were simply *motivated* to address the topics God cared about and get "close enough" in the details. We like to imagine that total accuracy goes without saying, but it does not; it would need to be stated emphatically in order to be biblically factual. And since we do find small problems all over the place, and the Bible never says otherwise, we could abandon the idea of the scriptures being perfectly accurate in all things. The fundamentalist will never do so.

MAYBE I'M THE ONLY one, but I can't help but notice that God *breathing* is different than God *speaking*. Breathing is generally silent, or indistinct. Why would Paul make up a word (*theopneustos*) specifically to emphasize something quiet and inarticulate like breath if his real point was to say that every word was given verbatim, like *speech*? Couldn't he have said that all scripture is *God-spoken* instead of *God-breathed* to be more accurate to what he meant? We know that Paul himself (while formerly known as Saul) *heard a voice* from Jesus on the road to Damascus, and he later recorded and recalled those words verbatim. It was not said that God breathed into Paul in order to write down the words of Jesus, but that he "heard" his "voice".

On this point, we can raise another problem. Even the story of Paul's conversion is not consistent, as a quick examination will show. Bible translations differ as to what Jesus told him. Some include a bit about Paul "kicking against the pricks" (Acts 9:5) in the initial exchange, while others don't. They all include it in his later recollection (Acts 26:14). Because some translations include it back into Acts 9:5, we get the impression that the translators might want to hide this inconsistency. If there's a discrepancy here, could the quotation of Jesus be *verbatim* in both cases? No, it could not. Both versions were told by the same man in the same book!

Furthermore, shouldn't we at least ponder whether Paul's quotation is "accurate" if Jesus was speaking Aramaic or Hebrew, but Paul wrote down his words only in Koine Greek, as we have it in the manuscripts of Acts? Are Christ's own words faithfully captured in the New Testament, or are they translated approximations? These questions are not easy, and they only compound.

SPEAKING OF HEBREW

Did you know that Hebrew lettering and grammar changed over time? Trying to sort out when the different scripts came into existence and how they morphed from one to the next is controversial and disputed, which should hardly be surprising considering how loaded the topic of the Bible and its claims are, and how long of a period it spans. From my research, this is one way to understand its possible evolution:

1. **Proto-Sinaitic**, a root script apparently adapted from Egyptian hieroglyphs and turned into an alphabet. Led to several other ancient alphabets as well.

2. **Paleo-Hebrew**, the oldest provable version with a direct link to Hebrew as it became known. What the Prophet Samuel and his school developed, influenced by Phoenician-Canaanite alphabet system.

3. **Classical Hebrew**, the version developed throughout the monarchies of David, Solomon and the kingdom of Judah, until the destruction of Solomon's Temple and their Babylonian exile.

4. **Late Biblical Hebrew**, the style influenced by Aramaic and Persian. Developed by Ezra the Scribe and subse-

quent writers of the post-exilic period for their new literature. (They still maintained Classical Hebrew for their existing holy scripture, but did not have Paleo-Hebrew writings anymore.)

5. **Amoraim Hebrew**, the version developed following the destruction of the Second Temple in 70 AD by rabbis to create new Talmudic texts. (Lasts for centuries.)

6. **Masoretic Hebrew**, the style used to standardize and unify the Tanakh, including pronunciation markings. (Only began around 600 AD.)

7. **Modern Hebrew**, the recreation of Classical/Late Biblical Hebrew by Eliezer ben Yehuda in the late 1800's. Many new words invented and old ones repurposed. (This is considered the language of Zionism and Israeli statehood, as opposed to Yiddish, which is considered the European bastard language.)

Paleo-Hebrew manuscripts of the Torah were to an extent maintained by the Samaritan tribes all the way up to modern day. If this is the case, couldn't God have protected the Paleo-Hebrew as the universal scripture of Jews everywhere, if it was closer to the original "inspired" work? Or if it was a good thing to change it, does that mean there was something wrong with it initially? Did it not matter that their Paleo-Hebrew "pictograph" style changed into foreign-looking alphabets over time? The oldest Hebrew script was long abandoned by the time of the Masoretes and their supposedly divine writing style. How could later languages, used by ungodly people, be an improvement over what God provided?

Note A -   Paleo-Hebrew fixation

SOME TODAY EVEN BELIEVE there is a magical property to Paleo-Hebrew that hides endless *secret meanings.* This view has grown in popularity among the uneducated.

You've probably never heard of the so-called "Berisheet Prophecy", but is has gone somewhat viral online in recent years, with the original video reaching almost 2 million views. It states that the very first word of the entire Hebrew Bible, *bereshit,* contains a hidden prophecy of the Son of God coming to be crucified on a cross for the salvation of sinners. Being a miracle of linguistic design, this is meant to fulfill what God meant when He said *"I declare <u>the end</u> from <u>the beginning</u>".* (Isaiah 46:10)

It's a wonderful idea. The beginning word of the Bible, which is the word "in the beginning" itself, and which was written in the very first language (ie. Paleo-Hebrew, if you believe that's what Adam and Eve spoke) to contain a striking prophecy about the Messiah, would be a miracle as amazing as the "Bible Code" of equidistant letter sequences. To reach such conclusion, the theorists creatively interpreted the visual aspect of the pictograph letters themselves (ie. a house, an ox, a hand, a tooth, etc.) and linked these pictures together in combinations to reveal more "hidden" meanings. No scholar would approve of this kind of stretched interpretation of a pictograph alphabet, but that doesn't stop them. Scholars say that the letters stopped carrying any inherent symbolic meaning at the moment when they were converted to convey a syllable sound rather than an image of a thing.[46]

---

46 For those wondering how this shift happened, it's not a unique process. Ancient languages started with spoken words, which were given pictures to directly symbolize them, so that the word for house was symbolized by

The video explaining it is an hour long, but has remarkable visual production to help people follow along, showing that a considerable amount of time, effort, and money was poured into it. It was published in 2018, and guarantees us that the Rapture of the Church will happen *before 2023*, on Rosh Hoshanah. Since that date has passed already, this makes it a false prophecy. But excuses will be made, and the game will go on.

Is Hebrew truly holy and distinct from all other languages, as some believe? If so, which version of Hebrew? Should it be the latest and most functional, or the earliest and most "pure"? Maybe something in between and temporary? If it is only the meaning of the words that matter, then the language does not matter, since words are only containers for meaning. But if it is truly sacred and distinct, and if God's hidden purposes are encrypted in the mystical interplay of whichever Hebrew letters are the real ones, we are all in very great danger of heresy and doom, as even Hebrew scholars could not tell us which version of Hebrew we are obligated to venerate.

Famously, Jesus Christ said (in Matthew 5:18), *"For assuredly, I say to you, until heaven and earth pass away, <u>one jot</u> or <u>one tittle</u> will by no means pass from the law until all is fulfilled."* Some fundamentalists use this saying as proof that not only did Jesus read the Hebrew scriptures in their original language and come to <u>uphold them</u>, but God upholds Creation itself with the

an actual drawing of a house. But eventually, after far too many things needed to be drawn and memorized, only the first syllable of the most common word-image pairs were kept, so that a house symbol did not represent an actual house anymore, but only the "h" sound, for instance. It still looked like a house pictograph, but it became nothing but a sound to be combined with other sounds, allowing endless combinations to make new words or sound out other ones. This is the shift from pictograph to alphabet in a nutshell.

120

Hebrew scriptures, as I've already mentioned. After all, they seem inextricably tied together here. Rabbinic Jewish philosophy says that Hebrew letters are exactly that: the building blocks of the universe, which have the power to reshape the cosmos when used correctly. They say, *"The letters of the Holy Tongue are the basic particles of the spiritual cosmic language."*.

> *The entire physical cosmos is a set of symbols corresponding to entities in the spiritual cosmos. The body of rules governing the manipulation of these symbols is what we call "Judaism" or here in this article "the Jewish way." ... Indeed, the Torah says that G-d [sic] created the universe by saying the specific words, "Let there be light... Let there be a firmament..." Each letter by itself has great significance. Letters can be combined into words, and the words into sentences, the sentences into paragraphs and so on. Each combination of letters, words and paragraphs possesses a unique significance and great potency in the spiritual realm. Each letter of the Hebrew alphabet is invested with many layers of meaning. The same is true with each word and each combination of words. Thus, each Hebrew prayer has many levels of meaning.'*
>
> *(Chabad.org. In their article 'The Cosmology of the Mitzvot')*

It goes on to explain how combined Hebrew prayers led by a holy man concentrate the energy of God and reorder the universe. '*Both performing and conducting, he leads a critical mass of at least ten soul-instrumentalists who create a spiritual symphony not only of overwhelming beauty but of powerful cosmic effect.*'

For some fundamentalists, this is exactly the kind of hyperbole they need. There is no limit to how far they will glorify

"Hebrew" (whatever that is), thinking that they are glorifying the Holy Tongue that may as well be the language of God. But for others, this reeks of a mad desperation to promote Hebrew supremacy over all other languages, in keeping with Zionist interpretation of what it means to be God's chosen people. Literally controlling the universe and the spiritual realm by praying and preaching in Modern Hebrew? That sounds like mankind giving itself the power of God.

Returning to what Jesus said, if we ignore the English (since it obviously came later), we are left with the Greek *iota* and *keraia*, not "jot" and "tittle". These are actually what we find in the New Testament text.[47] Therefore, it does not record the Hebrew equivalents, *yodh* and *tag*, which Bible teachers say is what Jesus *meant*. The Greek word *iota* derives from the *yod* of the Phoenicians, who were closely related to the Hebrews, and this word meant the same thing. In truth, all of these mean the same basic things, which are tiny letters and markings. But because Hebrew is considered magically important, certain groups can't accept the interchangeable nature of these sayings, because any disrespect against the Hebrew endangers the cosmos, which are dependent on the Tanakh to continue. They would refuse to believe that Jesus was actually referring to the Greek *iota* or *keraia*, even though that's what is written down.

Note B -   The name game

ALTHOUGH SURPRISING AND CONFUSING to many church leaders, millions of Christians today have become obsessed with rediscovering the "name of the Lord", claiming that "Jesus" is not

---

47 The New Testament recorded things in Greek no matter who was speaking or what they were saying, with very few exceptions.

122

just technically inaccurate to what his birth name was, but a dangerous and false invention that is unable to provide spiritual blessings when called upon. They say that his real name is *Yeshua*, which is a Hebrew name generally translated into Greek as *Iēsous*, which is what we find in the New Testament. Again, not *Yeshua*, but *Iēsous*, just as we find the word *iota* instead of *yodh*. There is no mention of *Yeshua* in the New Testament, because it was written in Greek and the names were presumably transliterated into their Greek equivalents. If this is confusing, just remember that this happens all the time today. The Spanish name Jorge is often transliterated into "George" in English, so a Mexican named Jorge who settles in an English community might end up being called George the rest of his life.

Those who follow "sacred name theology" reject this transliteration business completely. And they have valid reasons for doing so. They point to many verses which emphasize the name of the Lord as vitally important, such as:

> (John 14:14) *If you ask me anything <u>in my name</u>, I will do it.*

> (Acts 2:21) *And it shall come to pass that everyone who calls upon <u>the name of the Lord</u> shall be saved.'*

> (Romans 10:13) *For "everyone who calls on <u>the name of the Lord</u> will be saved."*

> (Philippians 2:9-11) *Therefore God has highly exalted him and bestowed on him <u>the name that is above every name</u>, so that <u>at the name of</u> [Yeshua?] every knee should bow, in heaven and on earth and under the earth, and every tongue confess that [Yeshua?] Christ is Lord, to the glory of God the Father.*

And there are many more verses besides these, which have similar teaching. Can we blame anyone for believing that this is a literal and direct teaching about the mystical power of the name of the Lord in its most exact sense? Just as people believe that "Yahweh" (or "Jehovah") is the real proper name of God the Father, which must not be taken in vain according to the 10 Commandments, the verbatim vowel sounds and lettering of the Lord is, in their understanding, more important than the person's intention of referring to him.

The Sacred Name Movement (SNM) was started by the Church of God (Adventist) denomination in the 1930s. Its goal was to emphasize the "Hebrew Roots" of Christianity, and undo the distortions introduced by the Romans and subsequent cultures, which obviously influenced the language and customs of Christianity, often for the negative. They believe the Messiah upheld a day of worship on the Sabbath, which is the seventh day of the week, as well as keeping Jewish festivals and food laws. The emphasis on Hebrew goes further, however, as some of their adherents claim the New Testament (ie. Greek manuscripts) is *invalid*, and that there must have been a long-lost Hebrew original text that was destroyed or secreted away! There is no evidence to support such a notion to begin with, and it would be the height of irony if God Almighty arranged such a thing to take place, but the retroactive logic of Hebrew mystics do not allow any obstacle to stand in the way of their premise. They rely on audacity and shock-value to inspire conformity, roping in those who have deep sensitivity to being rebuked and corrected by strongmen. They are sometimes called Judaizers, although they reject the authority and teachings of actual Jews, and make up their own version of Christianized Torah Law.

Increasingly, this movement is making the leap to claim that even the name *Yeshua* is not the proper name of the Lord, but only "Yahshua" or "Yahushua", since this neatly incorporates the "Yah" from "Yahweh". According to Semitic language experts this breaks the Hebrew rules of grammar and is obviously impossible, but this does not faze SNM proponents.

When we remember that the actual recorded name in the New Testament is the Greek *Iēsous*, and that *this particular name* is what is called sacred according to the text, it is even more baffling that groups would war about an imagined Hebrew root that is nowhere to be found. As far as I know, nobody suggests that *Iēsous* is the sacred name, or that Greek is the Holy Tongue.[48] Such is the mystical reputation of Hebrew.

THE IMPLICATIONS OF HOLY Tongue thinking and Sacred Name theology are deeply disturbing. Not only would we be missing key prophetic insights, and misunderstanding the blessed words of God, but thousands of years of Christianity will have been in vain, worshiping the wrong guy, saying the wrong prayers, and ensuring that Satan has the last laugh. It would only be this last generation of zealous (but incoherent) believers who somehow retrieved the key to God's Word. Their movement's success would be the only hope of restoring what the Lord intended, which is all the more tragic considering how badly they make their arguments. As with so many late-stage "discovery" theologies, one is forced to wonder why—if their claims are true—their

---

48 We might add the complication of Isaiah 7:14, which reads: *Therefore the Lord Himself will give you a sign: Behold, the virgin will conceive and bear a Son, and <u>shall call his name Immanuel</u>*. As it turned out, the virgin Mary did not call her son's name Immanuel. Matthew references this prophecy (in Mat 1:23) and interprets the fulfillment by pointing out that Immanuel translates to "God with us".

adherents are not receiving a pent up overflow of Holy Spirit blessings and spiritual gifts, since they would be the first to keep God's instructions correctly in almost two millennia! Instead, they are spreading hatred, division, legalism, and openly condemning "Jesus" and those who follow him.

As said, it is valid to bring up the many verses about the Lord's name to ask whether "Jesus" is the thing we should be saying in English. To make it even more curious, in English, a direct transliteration of *Yeshua* would be "Joshua", which is why we see *Iésous* rendered that way in our English New Testament.[49] Since we know the name of the historic character these passages refer to (Joshua, or *Yeshua*), it proves that the Jewish authors of the NT were willing to transform the Hebrew name *Yeshua* into the Greek *Iésous*, and thus it is reasonable that the name *Iésous* of our Lord was actually *Yeshua*. But this is not necessarily true, only a logical deduction based on the fairly safe assumption that Jews were still using Hebrew to name their children, and that God wanted His Son to have a Hebrew name, not a Greek one.

Could God possibly reject billions of Christians over thousands of years simply because of a naming mixup? I have watched social media personalities with millions of views emphatically declare that on Judgment Day, it will be so. *Yeshua* will look at everyone who innocently called on the name "Jesus" and condemn them outright. Can we even love such a God?

Here again, if the claims of these self-professed experts are true, God has some explaining to do. If the Hebrew name was so important to get literally correct, why would He not cause the authors of the New Testament to write *Yeshua* in the proper Hebrew characters at least once? Why couldn't the believers preserve the Hebrew manuscripts with the aid of the Holy

49 See Acts 7:45 and Hebrew 4:8.

126

Spirit? Why wait until the 1930s to reveal the truth, and then take another 80 years to propagate the message to a relatively minor subset of the faithful? Hebrew literacy remains so obscure that even in Jewish communities who attend synagogues and Torah schools it is rare to have students become proficient. Most Jews rely on rabbis and experts to make sense of the Hebrew. The same is true of Hebrew Roots followers, who do not actually understand the language themselves, but trust the authority of their organization. What a way for God to operate!

TARGUMS

Despite the supremacy of Hebrew in so many traditions, it is a fact that the Jews who were exiled to Babylon were quick to adopt the Aramaic script when they learned it. After their return to Jerusalem from Babylon, their holy texts were translated into proper Aramaic language. "Targum" simply means "translation" in Aramaic. This was not an adoption of the Aramaic script for the writing of Hebrew words, but an actual translation into a different (although related) language, like going from French to English. Few talk about the Targums anywhere, but they reveal a strange willingness to drift away from the Holy Tongue, even among the religious Jews.

Jews totally forgot how to speak or read Hebrew in the Persian empire. They loved and honored the Persians (especially king Cyrus) because he liberated them from Babylon and allowed them to return to Jerusalem to build a new temple. Persia had a policy of enforcing Aramaic language on their subjects, and Israel was no exception. Only a few experts, like Ezra the scribe, could translate the Hebrew into their (now native) tongue and make sense of what the Torah said.[50] This was not because Ezra loved Hebrew particularly, or was a prophet of God, but because

---

50 See Nehemiah 8.

scribes were obligated to copy Hebrew texts and understand them as scholars.

Jewish tradition (which often doesn't count for much) states that it was forbidden to write down Targums for some time after the restoration from Babylon, and that when the Targums were written they remained unsanctioned and non-authoritative at first. But whether it happened sooner or later, it happened. Targums became fully acceptable copies of biblical texts over time, and were allowed to be used in synagogues. Yemenite Jews still use the Targums in liturgy to this day. Modern Rabbinic traditions say that Jews should study the Hebrew twice and the Targums once (meaning a 2:1 ratio). That's a pretty strong endorsement for what could be considered a distortion of the Holy Tongue!

WHAT'S REMARKABLE, HOWEVER, IS that the Targums were not faithful and exact copies of the Hebrew. They included what scholars call "paraphrases", which is putting it lightly. These deviations can be quite shocking and notable. Extra details are added, and some verses are omitted. The term "Shekinah", for example, makes its appearance here, inserted into passages where it was not originally.[51]

We see the translation from Hebrew into Aramaic happening in the Bible itself when we look at the book of Nehemiah, where it says that Ezra "gave the sense, so that the people understood the reading" (Neh 8:8). This indicates translating and paraphrasing of some kind. They *rediscovered* Hebrew, as if it were a lost

---

51 Shekinah means the manifestation of God's presence on earth, such as appearing as fire, a cloud, or some other glory. Mysticism has further twisted the idea of Shekinah to mean the female aspect of God, and mystics claim to have a special relationship with it.

language. It may seem amazing what a generation or two can do to a tribe's culture, but remember that the whole reason why Jews were defeated and exiled in the first place is because God was furious with them for neglecting His Word for so many generations; implying that not even their forefathers in the old Jerusalem were literate, or at least not obedient, Torah followers.

Targums are thought to have influenced New Testament authors greatly, because their teachings incorporate logic found in the paraphrased parts. This makes it especially confusing for English readers of the Bible, because they have no access to the paraphrases, but can notice odd jumps from the way Jews talk from the Old Testament to the New.

In order to keep the Hebrew supremacy argument going, some have stated that Jesus was referring to the Targums themselves when he rebuked some Jewish leaders (in Mark 7:9-13) for replacing God's commands with human traditions. Perhaps this was part of the problem, but based on the examples given, it was clearly the Pharisees and scribes who had twisted scripture using their own "paraphrases" which went well beyond those found in the Targums.

Memra of YHWH

IN A FASCINATING TWIST, one of the major ways Targums deviate from the original Hebrew (if indeed it is a deviation) is by referring to the "Word of the Lord" (*Memra* of *YHWH*) whenever God had to do something anthropomorphic, such as make man in his image:

This comes as an astounding realization. The Targums say it was the Word of God who called down fiery judgments on the cities of Sodom and Gomorrah, for example, and the Word who made man in his image, and the Word who placed the burning coal on Jeremiah's lips. As a spirit, YHWH proper does not do human-like things, but his Word can. Considering that Jesus and the New Testament authors all agree on emphasizing the Word of God as a distinct and sometimes anthropomorphic expression of God Himself (as in John 1 and Colossians 1), both equal to the Father but not the same, this would suggest the Targums had serious weight in Jewish thought. It reveals the probability that the "paraphrased" translations are actually more faithful to reality, if not more faithful to some lost original Hebrew manuscripts, which the Masoretic Text failed to transmit. As bad as it sounds, the original Hebrew manuscripts may have had this language in them, and it could be that later scribes omitted them out of rebellion or ignorance.

IF THE THEOLOGY OF the Holy Tongue narrative is true, we would assume that every deviation from the pure Hebrew becomes less accurate, less sacred, and less influential on God's chosen people. Yet Jesus and his followers adopted innovations from the Aramaic Targums as legitimate revelations from God about Himself, despite these being absent from Hebrew texts and authored by people we don't even know about. Even if we presume that the Targums only said things already believed by the majority of the Jews by the time of their post-exile reconstruction period, where did these traditions come from? For all of their wanderings and unfaithfulness, at the end of the day weren't the Israelites people of the Book? How could such a bizarre tradition seep into the core of their teaching about God over time, to the point where they accepted new versions in new languages with new teachings?

STRANGER STILL TO THINK about, without the Targums and this "new" tradition, would the disciples of Jesus have had legitimate grounds to call him the living Word of God, and trace the activity of Christ back to so many places in the Old Testament? The monotheistic tenet of Israelite worship[52] is used as grounds for rejecting Jesus to this day, since Jews don't want to hear about God showing up as a human being who sweats, eats, defecates, and sleeps. The whole purpose of the Memra innovation seems to have been to distance the perfect Almighty God from anthropomorphism—not to draw attention to the fact that God could become human through His Word and live among us!

Does this also mean that the Targums should be considered canonical and pure? Should we update our Old Testaments to mention the Shekinah and Memra? Note that there are many changes besides these, and they do have implications we may not enjoy. In the first chapter of Genesis, for example, the Targum quite dramatically changes the narrative of the creation of the Sun and Moon. It states:[53]

---

52 Deuteronomy 6:4, compare to Mark 12:29
53 Found at: http://targum.info/pj/pjgen1-6.htm

132

And let them be for luminaries in the expanse of the heavens to give light upon the earth. And it was so. And the Lord made two great luminaries; <u>and they were equal in glory twenty and one years, less six hundred and two and seventy parts of an hour.</u> And afterwards <u>the moon recited against the sun a false report;</u> and she was diminished, and the sun was appointed to be the greater light to rule the day; and the moon to be the inferior light to rule in the night, and the stars. And the Lord ordained them unto their offices, in the expanse of the heavens, to give forth light upon the earth, and to minister by day and by night, to distinguish between the light of the day and the darkness of the night. And the Lord beheld that it was good. And it was evening, and it was morning, Day the Forth.

The Moon recited a false report against the Sun, and that's why it was the lesser of the two lights? This ascribes personality and history to the celestial lights beyond simply "ruling" their respective shifts. And what is with that strangely hyper-specific timing of them being "equal"? Scholars believe such details were improvised by Ezra or subsequent teachers in order to satisfy the questions of the ignorant Jews who took interest in the Torah after the exile. They asked questions, but since there was no answer in the book, somebody just made it up and ended up writing it down. But in this case, wouldn't it imply that the Shekinah and Memra innovations are also false? And doesn't this reduce the reliability of the New Testament which seems to adopt the Targums as legitimate in at least some ways?

Are we willing to accept this into our faith? How many changes like these need to be included before we reject the whole thing? Or are we willing to pick and choose which traditions we prefer? This is not a simple matter. God's Word is not to be trifled with, and such questions do not go away by simply dismissing them.

WHAT DID JESUS SAY?

Confusion is everywhere when it comes to language at the time of Christ, and this confusion is made worse by the absolute certainty of scholars who disagree about it! The New Testament was written in Koine (common) Greek by (mostly) Jews, but scholars agree that Jews spoke Aramaic first and foremost. That surprises some believers who only know about Hebrew, and assume that Jews would never lower themselves to speak something other than the Holy Tongue. But the academic world has long gotten used to it. Protestant churches are the ones who generally suggest the extreme view, being mostly ignorant about the existence of the Aramaic Targums or a Greek Old Testament to begin with. They prefer the Masoretic Text as the authoritative Old Testament, presumably perfect in its preservation of what God wanted us to know. There is reason to think otherwise.

We are told that Jesus spoke Aramaic. This is because the Gospels contain verses where Aramaic was recorded verbatim, rather than being "translated into Greek" like the rest of his words. These verses are Mark 5:41, 7:34, 14:36, and 15:34, as well as Matthew 26:47. This proves that Jesus did speak Aramaic at least some of the time. However, confusion about language is baked right into the text related to some of these verses, and raises questions that force us to think outside the traditional Protestant box, if that's where we come from.

We only need to compare Mathew 27:46 and Mark 15:34, where we have slightly differing accounts of what Jesus loudly cried out while he was on the cross. Both record his wording *exactly*, even going so far as to use the Aramaic script and being untranslated. Then the authors went out of their way to translate this Aramaic into Greek. In English, the phrase is said to mean, "My God, my God, why have you forsaken me?"

"Eli, Eli, lema sabachthani?" (Matthew 27:46)

Versus:

"Eloi, Eloi, lama sabachthani?" (Mark 15:34)

If you look closely, they're not exactly the same. It's important to realize that these differences are found in the Greek manuscripts, not just English translations. This is why our English translations reproduce the inconsistency *within the same Bible* – the King James Version will show that Matthew and Mark's accounts differ, for instance. Nobody believes that Jesus cried out two times with very slight alterations in his Aramaic phrasing, so this is an example of a biblical inconsistency.

But whichever version is correct, the statement by Jesus seems to be a based on Psalms 22:1, which would have been, in Hebrew:

Eli eli lama azavtani

Now you can see, this is a major departure from what either Matthew or Mark recorded. It rules out the possibility that Jesus quoted directly from the Hebrew Scriptures on the cross. All that remains would be the Aramaic Targum, we may assume. Not quite! Even the Targum is slightly different from what Jesus said:

Eli elahi metul ma shabaktani

Therefore, Jesus did not perfectly quote from *any Scriptures* here, but used Aramaic while paraphrasing.

Why? It might show a level of comfort he had with quoting Hebrew text as Aramaic speech. In other words, he may not have cared whether it was an exact quote from the Targums, because he actually studied the Hebrew and was simply trying to recite the verse roughly into Aramaic for his audience, which understood Aramaic far better than Hebrew.

Or perhaps Jesus had difficulty speaking clearly and in full sentences at all, due to the pain and strain of his crucifixion, after his horrific lashings. Or perhaps he was mentally confused by pain and blood loss. Or the witnesses couldn't agree on what was said, so that the authors who later transcribed their reports struggled to agree exactly, not because they heard what was said and forgot, but because conflicting testimony allowed both to be possible. In this case, of course, the Holy Spirit did nothing to straighten the matter out for them. None of these options give comfort to those who demand black-and-white confidence in the literal text. Fundamentalist assumptions about Bible stories don't hold up under critical examination, opening the door to disputes and divisions.

Confusion as proof

STRANGER YET, SCHOLARS POINT to these handful of Aramaic passages as proof that Jesus spoke Aramaic *primarily.* Despite the vast majority of his sayings being recorded in Greek in every account we have, they all assume the rare exceptions should inform the rest of the text, and not the other way around. Even a child should understand how silly this assumption is. If I were to utter French phrases occasionally to people who understood French expressions but did not normally speak it, would it be logical for later historians to assume I always spoke French when looking at transcripts of what I say? If the majority of my speeches are recorded in English, why wouldn't they conclude that I'm primarily an English speaker? Why would the New Testament authors suddenly stop to record one or two Aramaic sentences verbatim? According to the prevailing view, they translated everything else that Jesus said into Greek from Aramaic, so why not do it all or nothing? And why go on to give the Greek equivalent next to them, as if the readers would not understand the Aramaic if it was left verbatim? If they spoke Aramaic as their native tongue and were literate at all, wouldn't they know how to read Aramaic and not need the Greek translation?

Another view is that Koine Greek was used exclusively for the benefit of the Gentile foreigners, who were beginning to seek accounts of the stories; these stories were already accepted and known in the Jewish world, because they centered on Jerusalem. If that were the case, it is alarming that the Jews did not insist on having a full Aramaic record produced first, for posterity. We would expect that portions of the Aramaic source documents would be translated into Greek for the sake of the Gentile believers abroad. Did the authors of the New Testament hate the Jews so much for killing Jesus that they refused to write in their preferred languages (either Hebrew or Aramaic)? Considering that Paul, who was the ambassador to the Gentiles, loved his fellow Israelites enough to wish he could die in their place, this is unlikely.[54] If the Greek writings were meant exclusively for Gentiles who had no knowledge of Jewish customs and prophecies, then why are the Gospels not full of lessons that the Gentiles would need to understand in order to understand the significance of what Jesus was accomplishing? The choice of their quotations from him, and the surrounding commentary, is clearly written as if the intended audience is Jewish, and would have some grasp of their prophecies. There aren't comparisons to Greek deities or philosophers, but reminders about Israelite scriptures. It really seems that the audience was Jewish, but spoke Koine Greek. And if that's the case, what did Jesus speak?

IF ANYTHING, THE STRANGE inclusion of Aramaic phrases proves that Jesus did *not* speak Aramaic normally, which is why the authors made a special note of those occasions when he did!

> *When some of those standing nearby heard this, they said, "Behold, he is calling for Elijah."*
>
> *(Mark 15:35)*

This is the kicker. Not even the people standing around Jesus at the cross understood what his words meant. Biblical accounts say Jesus "cried out in a loud voice", meaning he was not whispering or muttering; so that couldn't have been the reason they were confused. We know that his actual meaning was, "My

---

54 Romans 9:3

God, my God, why have you forsaken me?" but why wouldn't Aramaic-speaking people understand him? They thought he was calling out for the prophet Elijah for some reason—perhaps truncating his name to "Eli" instead. But if the real meaning of "Eli" was "my God" in Aramaic (which is what the authors themselves tell us) then why would anyone not recognize that?

There was a language barrier even among Jews when he spoke Aramaic. We can assume the bystanders were Jewish, since Gentiles would not know Elijah's story well enough to remember he was taken to heaven instead of dying, and could therefore return and help Jesus on the cross.

Then again, Jesus probably had an accent because he was from Galilee, which had a distinct dialect. We know that Peter had a distinct accent (from Matthew 26:73) because he was a fisherman from Galilee as well, and could not hide it. Repeated insults and surprise about the possibility of the Messiah being from the Galilean region can be found throughout the Gospels, and this could be part of the reason why Jesus spoke differently and was misunderstood on the cross. Would his dialect be different enough for him to incorrectly recite the Psalm? How many other times was Jesus misunderstood while speaking Aramaic to other Aramaic-speaking people? None that I see.

Logically, even as a choice to include in the narrative, it makes little sense to point out that the listeners did not understand Jesus at that moment. It's not as if this confusion leads to important developments later on. Instead, it seems to be a payoff for something already notable and worthy to mention; namely, an abnormal decision to loudly quote an Aramaic verse to them, in a language they were not so fluent in. This alone may explain why the witnesses were surprised enough to insist on his exact wording being recorded verbatim in Aramaic, with a Greek translation provided. It also explains why their confusion would have been both natural and worth pointing out for the record. Perhaps they wanted to emphasize the boldness of the Lord's decision to cry out in Aramaic despite the risk of being misunderstood. As for why Jesus would not have used Greek to express himself if that was his primary language, by quoting the Septuagint perhaps, is yet another mystery. Perhaps he wanted to conceal his meaning from the majority of those who stood and watched, but ensure that some of them did their homework and figured out the reference, and what it meant. If he had said it plainly in Greek, they might have thought he was actually being abandoned by God, and not quoting a Psalm which clearly points to him being the Messiah.

PEOPLE TODAY LOVE to translate Christ's words "back into Hebrew" or "back into Aramaic" in order to unlock the "real" meaning of what he said. But isn't this presumptuous and dangerous? If God's Word is sacred, and if exactitude is a virtue when studying it, how can anyone presume that the entire New Testament would be recorded in a language that does not accurately capture the facts of what was said by the Lord, whose words are the very source of life we depend on?

For example, did Jesus actually state (in Revelation 1:8, 21:6, and 22:13) that he was the "Alpha and the Omega" (ie. the first and last letters of the *Greek* alphabet), or did he say he was the "Aleph and the Tav" (ie. the first and last letters of the *Hebrew* alphabet)?[55] According to every old manuscript, he used the *Greek* letters. What should we trust: the text itself, or scholarly

---

55 A third possibility: Jesus spoke what scholars consider to be his native tongue. This would mean he said the Aramaic "Alaph" and "Taw", which is closely related to Hebrew, but not the same.

deductions? Common sense, or Jewish tradition? What does God want us to believe? This problem infuriates Hebrew elitists and confuses fundamentalists. Why couldn't it just be simple?

SEPTUAGINT

THE SEPTUAGINT SHEDS LIGHT, but only on a bigger mess.

The story goes like this. 336 years before Christ, a great military leader named Alexander the Macedonian began to conquer the world. While invading the Middle East, Asia, and Africa he constructed more things than he destroyed. He founded the coastal city of Alexandria (named after himself) in northern Egypt, which would go on to be one of the greatest cities of the Mediterranean world. This city housed the world's most advanced library of rare texts; these were translated into Greek for his people to study. The Greeks loved history, and saw themselves as the historians of the world. Alexander only reigned for 13 years before dying, but his army reached as far as India. Even while alive, legends spread about him everywhere, and local pagan priests were known to greet him as if he were a god on his arrival, not an evil threat. He crushed Darius the Mede, which spelled the end of the Persians and paved the way for Greek takeover everywhere they had ruled.

The Persian empire had adopted Aramaic as their official language in order to unite their various subjects, but Alexander and his generals would go even farther. Their plan changed the course of Western history. Persian unity led to the creation of the Aramaic Targums, but Greek unity would leave an even bigger impact called "Hellenization". The Greek Old Testament, known as the Septuagint, was only one of the major byproducts of Hellenization, and its role has not been appreciated.

THE JEWS ACTUALLY SUBMITTED to Alexander's conquest. They peacefully allowed him and his armies to pass through their land, like many other tribes did. This is why Alexander conquered places so quickly. Alexander, for his part, took no interest in the city of Jerusalem or their Jewish customs, since they were not important to his ambition. He passed them by along the Mediterranean Sea coastline, not bothering to go up into their mountains. When he destroyed the Persians who governed Israel, he simply replaced Persian officials with Greek ones, allowing Jews to keep their practices and privileges. It was a change of management, you could say. After his death Alexander was revered, not despised, by the Jews. How revered? Enough that Jewish legends claim that Alexander had a special meeting by their High Priest, which impressed him so much that he stopped to bow to the name of the Lord, which was written on the breastplate of the High Priest. In their tale, Alexander recognized the High Priest from one of his dreams, as a prophet who spurred him on to conquer in the first place! He personally visited the Temple and made an offering to God. All of this is quite comical, since Alexander thought himself to be a god, and spared little time along his war path. Plus, the only account of this legend is from the Jewish historian Flavius Josephus, hundreds of years later. This shows just how popular Alexander remained, but also how the legend stuck around and became conflated with factual history.

144

The Jews wanted to elevate their nation's prestige, and they did so by saying they were worthy of Alexander's honor on a religious level. They wanted to connect themselves with a pagan Greek conqueror!

A different strategy came from the Samaritans, whom you may recall kept their own version of the original Paleo-Hebrew Torah. They were Jerusalem's old relatives to the north, the remnants of the ten tribes who were defeated by the Assyrians. They brokered peace with Alexander in exchange for permission to build their own temple to Yahweh in Mount Gerizim. Unfortunately, when the existing governor who brokered this deal died of natural causes, Alexander sent a replacement for him, who was then burned alive by the Samaritans! That was a big mistake. Alexander had no choice but to send his army to destroy the city. The stigma surrounding the Samaritans by the time of Jesus' ministry may have been, in part, due to their rudeness toward Alexander the Great centuries earlier. He was not only admired by Jews for centuries during the Hellenization period, but also during Rome's subsequent conquest. Rome also adored Alexander, just as historians still do to this day. He put past conquerors to shame with the scale of his accomplishments, and by the logic of the ancient world, this could only be possible by the blessing of the heavens; legitimizing not only his territorial claims, but his vision for the world.

New identity, new translation

ALEXANDER'S HELLENIZATION STRATEGY WAS startling and unprecedented, although it would be imitated countless times by future conquerors. He ordered entire cities to be built from the ground up in remote places and married local princesses to his underlings. He had his soldiers take conquered women as wives and produce children who would be educated in the Greek way. Scholars say 10,000 children were born due to this strategy during his short reign alone, not to mention generations born in the wake of this mingling. Alexander himself had been taught by the genius Greek philosopher Aristotle, and Hellenization was therefore an extension of a new kind of Greek empirical superiority of mind and body. They believed they were the pinnacle of mankind, so that rather than wanting to plunder and oppress the "barbarians" (as they called everyone who wasn't Greek) they wanted to enlighten the world with the divine gift of Greek society. This impulse to enlighten the world was the core of Hellenism.

The death of Alexander at the young age of 32 was followed by division and war. He never chose a successor, and his sons (who were never legitimized) were assassinated quickly. His four generals divided up the realm and fought for supremacy. The two winners straddled Israel to the north and south—with both claiming to be the successor, and both aggressively Hellenizing to prove it. The cities they constructed featured temples for Greek gods, gymnasiums for sports and education, council buildings, and other famously Greek institutions which promoted their brand of dignity. They celebrated art, philosophy, and of course Greek language itself. Integration became essential for skilled workers who traveled and signed contracts, regardless of their heritage, ethnicity, or religion.

THE CITY OF JERUSALEM, though initially impressed by Alexander himself, became a battleground in the war between his generals. It was first captured by the southern king, Ptolemy, who carried off many Jews to Egypt as captives. This may sound like another terrible recreation of the Babylonian incident, but it wasn't so bad. The scribes, scholars, and workmen who were transported to Alexandria ended up seeing it as an upgrade. Alexandria was, after all, a wonder of the world, with specially aligned roads that drew coastal breezes through the streets for miles, and the great library that it became famous for. The reason why Alexander named this city after himself was because it was meant to be the fountainhead of Hellenization. Its great library would be key to ensuring Greek influence continuing to spread long after his reign. Their library ensured that the Greeks, despite being superior, were not only able to understand their conquered subjects, but integrate ideas from them and produce new philosophies. It was a syncretic melting pot, but with Greeks dominating; a tactic that would be used by Romans later. The proud capital of Athens was across the Mediterranean Sea, but it was Alexandria which became the new source of Greek influence.[56]

Unlike the forced labor and hardship in the days of Moses, this Egyptian captivity was loved by the Jews as an escape from their unhappy homeland. They were treated well, given respectable occupations, and assimilated.[57] Jewish identity was rapidly being erased, and scholars say it nearly went extinct along with the Hebrew language. And not just in Alexandria. Israelites every-

---

56 When you hear about "Egyptian" or "Coptic" influence after this point in history, know that it refers to this Hellenistic headquarters of Greek fame, not the Bronze Age Egyptians Moses dealt with.

57 In a way this is also what happened in Babylon, under Nebuchadnezzar. Babylon had an impact on Jewish thought. But at that time, the trauma and devastation of losing the temple and Holy City made it hateful, not welcome. Greek capture was considered good, which is why they ended up glorifying Alexander in their legends.

where, including Samaritans, were being "converted". Jews named their children Greek names, enjoyed Greek literature, and some even participated in Greek nude wrestling, which was the popular sport. Jews born across Israel were raised to speak Greek as their mother tongue—not Hebrew, and not Aramaic! That shouldn't be surprising, but to most Christians it would be taken as lunacy because our church historians have practically erased the world-changing culture shift that took place under Hellenism. They focus instead on the Babylonians, Persians, and Romans, pretending that the Greeks are a footnote, probably because it's embarrassing.

IN ALEXANDRIA, AROUND 250 BC, long before the Hasmonean Dynasty took over Jerusalem and created an independent Jewish kingdom again, an official Greek translation of the Hebrew Torah was requested by Ptolemy the Great, the Greek king of Egypt and son of one of Alexander's generals. It was commissioned so that Jewish literature could be preserved and accessed in the famous Greek library there. This was predictable, since the Greeks were interested in gathering all of the rare ancient texts and understanding their secrets (which helped to rule them).

Legend says the initial translation work was done by 72 experts of Hebrew who traveled from Jerusalem upon request. Despite being kept in their own quarters – each with the same Hebrew scrolls, but kept apart from each other – they each quickly and separately produced perfectly identical translations into Koine Greek. Unlike the older, more difficult and formal dialects of Greek (of which there were several), Koine was the language of Hellenism, and therefore of everyday use by everyone. To have the Torah in the universal language of the day was

148

a marvel, a celebration, and a new era of Jewish thought, able to freely communicate with Greek people about faith and God.

But what does the translation story reveal? Not only does it tell us that there were at least seventy Jewish experts who were religious and knew Koine Greek very well in Israel, but that they were ready to be summoned to a foreign kingdom to do this work. They had no religious or intellectual objection to it. It would have caused a memorable incident if they had refused. But they were not too snobby or racist to translate God's Word into that of pagans. Also, their amazing success gave the distinct sense that the enterprise had been a miracle of God Himself, proving that the God of Abraham, Isaac, and Jacob also blessed the Greek language becoming a staple of Jewish religious discourse. That idea spoke volumes, since Jews in particular always watched for signs and evidence from God, rather than logic.[58]

It was this legend of the perfect translation that eventually gave birth to the Latin name "Septuagint", or "LXX", since *septuaginta* meant 70 in Latin, and *LXX* is the Roman numeral for 70. In reality, regardless of what initially occurred, there would end up being variations in Greek translations after this point, especially as the scope expanded from the first five books of the Bible to the rest of the Old Testament as we know it.

AFTER THE INITIAL TRANSLATION of the Torah, the rest of the books we would recognize from the Old Testament were translated into Greek as well, and were widely available during the time of the Jewish Hasmonean Dynasty that would come later. It was popular among the highest and lowest of Jews, since God

---

58 *For Jews always ask for signs, but Greeks search reason; (1Cor 1:22)*

Himself had apparently blessed its creation. It was respected for being faithful to the Hebrew way of thinking while also improving one's understanding. It did not respect the Aramaic Targum "paraphrase" choices, however, showing that the additions of the Targums were probably not in the oldest Hebrew scrolls. Pronunciations, expressions, and organization were all improved by Koine Greek, not diminished. With knowledge of the Torah spreading in Greek, people's hunger for the Messiah and His Kingdom grew steadily. Critically, the prophetic book of Daniel was eventually translated into the Greek scriptures, which certainly seemed to prophesy about the rise of Alexander, the division of his kingdom by his four generals, the Greek empire's greatness, but also its downfall and the arrival of the Jewish Messiah.

The Targums had already set the precedent of popular translations for average believers, but they lacked the same credibility as this. The excitement over the Septuagint and its acceptance into the Alexandrian library was a cause of celebration. Synagogues (which derive their name from the Greek word *synagōgé*, meaning "assembly") embraced the text. For once, the entire history of Israel and their God would be open for the pagan world to learn about.

Strikingly, it is the Greek Old Testament—not the Hebrew, nor the Targums—that is most often quoted directly in the New Testament. Jesus and the disciples use the Greek Old Testament to make their points and teach prophecy. This proves that it was considered authoritative by Paul and the other disciples. Some of the New Testament authors were more eloquent in writing Greek, such as Matthew (the Jewish tax collector working for Rome) and especially Luke (the Gentile physician who studied under Paul), while others had only a fundamental and practical

150

understanding of the language, such as Peter (the uneducated fisherman) yet they were all fluent. Clearly the language was popular among even religious Jews!

Despite the Septuagint—or perhaps because of it—Jewish identity was not lost. It was preserved throughout the turbulence of the wars and rebellions because the Scriptures were available and understandable.

HELLENISM REMAINED CONTROVERSIAL BECAUSE it represented a rejection of Jewish pride. "Hellenists" are mentioned by name in Acts 6:1 and Acts 9:29 as a group that Paul disputed with; in fact, they sought to kill him, forcing him to escape the city of Jerusalem with the help of others. Jewish Christians who read, wrote, and spoke Greek did not consider themselves to be Hellenists, since that implied a change of core identity, not just language adoption. Hellenist Jews were anti-Christian because they didn't believe in the Torah or Christ as important, and wanted to remain as protected Greek subjects. Yet some English translations hide the term from the reader, as in the KJV, which says "Grecians", while the New Living Translation says "Greek-speaking Jews". Others says "Hellenistic Jews", but even in this case the implications are unclear. Was speaking Greek as your primary language all that it took to be considered an outsider, worthy of a special label compared to a normal Jew? Or were these men personally devoted to Greek religion as well—which was certainly the hope of the Greek rulers?

Jewish rebellion and royalty

OVER A CENTURY AFTER the Septuagint was popularized, while Alexandria yet spread its charms from Egypt, its aggressive counterpart to the north—which became the much larger Seleucid Empire, with Antioch as its capital—would take over Jerusalem by force and show intolerance toward Jewish practices. They did not have a great library and propaganda to seduce the people, they had authority, power, and vast numbers.

We can't know if Hellenistic persecution of Torah-practicing Jews is what triggered the revolt, or if their increasing revolts are what triggered persecution, escalating into violence, but civil war erupted between traditionalist Jews and Hellenists. Interestingly, the most detailed accounts of this conflict come from the books of Maccabees, which ended up in Greek versions of the Jewish scriptures,[59] although they are not considered divinely inspired even by Jews, and doubtlessly served as propaganda. Their accounts of the civil war and the particular behaviors of Seleucid emperor Antiochus IV Epiphanes are almost certainly inaccurate as a result.

By some accounts, Antiochus IV Epiphanes did not even realize what was going on until tax revenue for the region dried up, and attacked the city as revenge, looting the temple to reclaim lost money and perhaps defiling it in some way for good measure. Forbidding the practice of circumcision and other Jewish rites was a further humiliation meant to erase their culture and replace it with a more fully realized Hellenism. This

---

59 "The Septuagint" normally gets applied to all Jewish literature translated into Greek, but the actual work of the 72 scholars (if that legend is true) was only for the first five books of the Torah. Everything that came later was translated and incorporated piece by piece.

152

galvanized the Jews and stoked the flames. Some wished to stay and give up their Jewish identity, while the devout traditionalists spurred on a larger majority to accept a new dynasty and declare independence from both Antioch and Alexandria. The Maccabees books were important for promoting their own lopsided version of events, which would help legitimize their strange claim to the throne of David.

Maccabees frames the revolt as fulfillment of Daniel's prophecies, leading to their own Messianic efforts. They believed the hostility of Antiochus fulfilled the "abomination of desolation" prophecy, and many today buy into this idea. It raises the question of why Jesus would clearly refer to it as a future event (in Mark 13:14). In reply, Bible teachers often employ the idea of "typology" and "prophetic foreshadowing", so that they don't have to admit that the Maccabean version of history was probably a lie, meant to prop up a bloodthirsty usurping family. They did not conform to the Law of Moses or the Davidic lineage, after all. They wanted to be seen as a band of heroes blessed by God.

In any case, a new day dawned on Jerusalem. Under the leadership of one family of Jewish zealots, the traditionalists fought hard, sacrificed much, and eventually emerged victorious. It was the rise of a violent, proud, peculiar, poorly educated, and legally unqualified Jewish family. This was the start of the Hasmonean Dynasty.

Their reign lasted several generations but had many internal issues, inviting further invasions by the Seleucids, and weakening their power. In 63 BC, the Jewish Queen "Alexandra" Salome made an alliance with the sect known as the Pharisees, and agreed to promote their order to a position of power. Pharisees would govern Jewish law on a dangerous new level.

THE PHARISEES WERE SCRIBES and legal scholars, but compared to the upper class priesthood known as the Sadducees they were popular, because they made themselves available and taught often; even if their doctrine turned out to be bad. The Sadducees were elitists who ignored the daily needs of Jews, concerning themselves only with maintaining the Temple and performing its sacred rituals, as well as punishing those who broke Torah laws. The choice of Queen Alexandra to hand decision-making power to the Pharisees would prove a fateful one indeed.

Clearly, Hellenism had provoked the rise of the Hasmoneans, but this did not mean Queen Alexandra felt the need to respect the priesthood, which represented the traditional Torah system. The Sadducees retained official power over the Temple and had their own soldiers, and were still necessary for sin atonement and appeasing God, but she consulted the Pharisees even on matters of state. They effectively became Jerusalem's administrators, leaving the lofty Sadducees as a ceremonial relic more than a governing force. Why did she abandon the roots of the religious government in favor of the scholars? Because in order to truly be independent there needed to be a cultural revolution, not just a dynasty of Jews in power. Hellenism, which undermined Jewish identity and the traditionalist cause of the Hasmoneans, was widespread, and could not be replaced by royal decree. It had to be skillfully replaced by a new culture that only the Pharisees were shrewd enough to sow and harvest.

The internal problems of the Hasmoneans were evident to all, leading to fights over succession and appointed roles. The victories of the Greek invaders proved that God was not really on the side of the traditionalists after all. Jewish diehards pushed for Aramaic-influenced Late Hebrew as a language, and minted coins with Hebrew on it as if to prove that they were true to their roots. But these were superficial attempts to undo centuries of Greek dominance, and did not replace the *lingua franca*. Also, the Septuagint proved too popular to get rid of. Greek was not only practical, but it had a richness for details and big ideas. Even the Jewish leaders of the war against the Hellenists ended up employing Koine Greek to communicate in urgent situations – because Aramaic and Hebrew were far too inefficient and unclear. When it really mattered, Greek won every time.

The false kingdom crumbles, the real kingdom arrives

THE PHARISEES WERE SHREWD indeed, and knew that restoring the original Torah practices was impossible. They, of all people, being the legal scholars, did not want to be tasked with turning Hellenized Jews back to the arcane system which had defeated the great patriarchs and led to God's judgment! The people could read the Greek scriptures perfectly well, but it was necessary to convince them that the Hebrew (which they could not read) held encoded truths, and that there was an "Oral Law" never written down which decoded these mysteries. Because of this charade, it became necessary for ordinary people to obey strange new traditions that would rule out the need to obey the literal Torah as written. They called this making "a fence around the Law".

For the Pharisees and Queen Salome Alexandra, their dynasty was about political independence, not a real return to Moses or David. They knew that their kingdom would not survive by God's blessing; they had to take matters into their own hands.

Eventually, during a time of strife between Queen Alexandra's heirs, the Pharisees advised both of the rivals to call upon Rome for aid. Thus, the Roman general Pompey answered the call, but in the way you might expect a Roman ruler to approach the problem: he conquered the city and declared the end of the Hasmonean dynasty once and for all, just as the Pharisees planned. Israel's independence was lost again, eliminating any remaining hope that they were the Kingdom of God spoken of in Daniel's prophecy.

KNOWING ALL OF THIS, it is nonsensical to imagine that Jews did not regularly use Greek language at the time of Jesus, even if some high-minded scholars resented its usage and wished to revive Hebrew to prove that they hadn't totally lost their heritage. The fact that Gospels and letters were meant to be read aloud, verbatim, to crowds who were largely Jewish, means that the choice to write in Koine Greek reflects the common tongue of Jews at this time. This was the same language as the popular Septuagint, which they'd loved for so long. It was the Pharisees who wished to downplay the Septuagint, mystify the Hebrew, and convince the Jews that they were gravely mistaken about how to interpret scripture. They, the legal experts and masters of the Hebrew texts, having been legitimized by the queen herself, would decide what God meant! The choice of the New Testament authors to write exclusively in Koine Greek was a statement about their refusal to let the Pharisees gatekeep God's Word any longer. They wanted to ensure that the average Jew could understand the message clearly and communicate with Gentiles about it.

How fascinating that Jesus arrives at this particular junction, which was a crossroads of language and politics, where the balance of power was weak on all sides. He attacked the Pharisees as hypocrites, actors, false leaders, and exposed their evil in front of the common people. He brought a dramatically different understanding of the Torah to the masses, and created hope of a new covenant that would make the Pharisees and their obsession with the Law obsolete. The Pharisees had teamed up with Rome since the beginning, acting as the cultural manipulators of the subjected Jews, ensuring the flow of taxes to Rome while always trying to negotiate and advocate a better arrangement. Jesus represented an existential threat to their prestige, their invented traditions, their Hebrew mystification (Jesus and his disciples quoted the Septuagint, not the Hebrew), and their hidden agenda. The Sadducees remained stubborn, out of touch, and culturally irrelevant while holding impressive titles that gave them more direct access to Roman officials, as well as the power to condemn, arrest, and sentence law-breakers.

Early Jewish believers multiplied the Greek writings of the disciples, copying and spreading them from city to city, evangelizing with them even under persecution from Pharisaic devotees and Roman pagans. They wanted to spread the Word as far as possible using the *lingua franca* of the world. The Good News of the Kingdom of God was never meant to be limited to one ethnicity. Only Greek made Christianity's spread possible.

Logic reinforces this. Do we imagine that preachers were expected to hold the Greek document in their hands and verbalize it in Aramaic for the people? Likewise, do we imagine that the witnesses who walked with Jesus recorded his blessed words —the words of the long-awaited Messiah, the only-begotten Son of God!—in another language than what he spoke? Did they care nothing about preserving his true Aramaic sayings, parables, and phrases, except in a few random cases? Can we really humor the idea they all spoke and heard his teachings in Aramaic, translated them into written Greek, used the Septuagint's phrasing for their scriptural quotations, and yet expected everything to be translated back into Aramaic for future listeners? If nothing else, the burden of proof is on those who believe this, and they have no proof.

We know that Jesus was killed by the Pharisees and Sadducees together, who ruled Jerusalem through the Sanhedrin council. The unbelieving Jewish intellectuals *disowned the Septuagint* eventually, in order to keep a grip on Scripture and maintain Hebrew as their theological tongue, which Christians were not accustomed to and therefore could not argue against effectively. Therefore, they concocted what became the Masoretic Text in order to counter the use of the Septuagint, claiming that their Hebrew text was pure and accurate, while the Greek text (now associated with Christianity) had turned out to be unreliable after all, despite being celebrated as a divine work early on.

> *The oldest and most important of all the versions made by Jews is that called "The Septuagint" ... Its influence upon the Greek-speaking Jews must have been great. In course of time it came to be the canonical Greek Bible. ... Two things, however, rendered the Septuagint <u>unwelcome in the long run</u> [ie. after Christ] to the Jews. Its divergence from <u>the accepted text (afterward called the Masoretic)</u> was too evident; and it therefore could not serve as a basis for theological discussion or for homiletic interpretation. This distrust was accentuated by the fact that it had been <u>adopted as Sacred Scripture by the new faith</u> [ie. Christianity]. A revision in the sense of the canonical Jewish text was necessary.*

The Septuagint pointed to Jesus Christ, which is why the New Testament writings clearly use it for their theological arguments, but the Pharisees who took control of Judaism wanted to shield their followers from its messianic messages, and so they insisted on a Hebrew text that they controlled exclusively. How much tampering was introduced by these scholars has been a matter of debate since its earliest days, with Christian apologists arguing that the Rabbinic Jews found many ways to undermine specific Christian arguments of their day which relied on the Greek Septuagint translation. When they would point out verses to Jews, they would take it to their Rabbis, who would show them the Masoretic Text as proof that it was all a misunderstanding (or worse) on the part of the Christians. How far from the nice assumptions of the fundamentalist Protestants who love their King James Bible, which bases its Old Testament translation on the Masoretic Text!

These rabbinic leaders also hated Gentiles. An influx of non-Jews learning the Old Testament was anything but welcome! It infuriated them, since their false traditions could be exposed and their hypocrisy easily detected. We can't know whether the Septuagint (which began as the first five books of the Bible, but eventually included everything, including some Apocrypha) was ever the best translation, but it was good enough for Jesus Christ and the authors of the New Testament, who had the Holy Spirit.

THIS IS ALSO WHY PAUL (who had been a Christian-murdering Pharisee, named Saul) understood the danger the Pharisees

---

60 https://www.jewishencyclopedia.com/articles/13432-septuagint

posed and the lengths they would go to. He influenced Luke, a Gentile believer, who thoroughly investigated the claims surrounding Jesus' life in order to write his Gospel. Paul wanted to ensure that Jews were not exclusively relied upon as the leaders of Christianity. Luke included more examples of the Pharisees fighting Jesus (and vice versa) than anyone else, and this is not a coincidence. Paul knew all about their schemes and worked overtime to counter their efforts, establishing Jesus as the rightful Messiah by quoting the Greek Septuagint and elucidating the prophetic connections.

As we continue to look more closely at the myriad claims of scholars, mystics, and religious institutions, it is important to remember the world-changing implications of language. It is not only the details, which may affect our souls, but the minds of the masses and the systems of control which depend on the careful use of language and perception.

LOST BOOKS

I ALWAYS ASSUMED THAT the writings of Solomon had been treated like golden treasures to Israelite people, since we are told how foreign kings and queens from around the world came to seek his wisdom. But the Bible itself shows us that many of his writings failed to survive. They must have been poorly managed in the decline of the kingdom and its divisions, with heretical kings not bothering to make copies of them, or they may have been destroyed, lost, or stolen when they were conquered by pagans. Look at how many writings Solomon produced:

> *He also spoke 3,000 proverbs, and his songs were 1,005. He spoke of trees, from the cedar that is in Lebanon to the hyssop that grows out of the wall. He spoke also of beasts, and of birds, and of reptiles, and of fish. And people of all nations came to hear the wisdom of Solomon, and from all the kings of the earth, who had heard of his wisdom.*
>
> *(1 Kings 4:32-34, English Standard Version)*

Do we have a thousand songs from Solomon? Not even close. We have one song, called "Song of Songs" or "Song of Solomon."

Obviously his writings were not respected as much as one might assume!

It gets worse. In 2 Chronicles[61] it says the following:

> *Now the rest of the acts of Solomon, <u>first and last,</u> are they not written in the history of Nathan the prophet, and in the prophecy of Ahijah the Shilonite, and in the visions of Iddo the seer concerning Jeroboam the son of Nebat?*
>
> *(2 Chronicles 9:29, English Revised Version)*

What's incredible is that all of these books became lost.

THE DESCRIPTION SAYS "first and last", evidently referring to the earliest and latest periods of Solomon's life, or possibly meaning certain aspects spanning from beginning to end. By saying this, the authors of 2 Chronicles acknowledge that their records do not include many stories of Solomon. Several other verses in the book tell us that the rest of the deeds of a certain king are found in the annals of the kings of Israel—meaning, the books of 1 Kings and 2 Kings, which were written earlier—but Solomon's missing stories are notably different and unique, suggesting that not only did the normal annals not suffice, but special documents were required to fill in the blanks that they still had on hand. Therefore, the Bible's story about Solomon is provably incomplete in a major way.

We are missing the history of Nathan the Prophet, the prophecies of Ahijah, and the visions of Iddo the Seer. They all went extinct some time after 2 Chronicles was written, but before the

---

61 2 Chronicles was composed from a long history of records, but only finalized after the Babylonian exile, as we see by the fact that it concludes with the liberation of the Jews from Babylon by Persian king Cyrus.

Targums or Septuagint were translated. This is strange and tragic. They survived long enough to be referenced by the post-Babylonian Jews, but did not make it into the collection eventually called the Tanakh. No copies exist anywhere today, and nobody knows what they said, including Jews.

Think of what we might have learned! Clearly, the writers of 2 Chronicles were familiar with these works, and counted them as substantial records which each deserved their own recommendations. That means they were truthful and contained vital information, and must have been in the royal library of the Second Temple for some time. They might have included hundreds of important details that would reinforce the legitimacy of Ecclesiastes as Solomon's work, and taught us crucial connections between him and foreign civilizations, for example. Perhaps these cultures, including the nascent Greeks, would go on to use Solomon's ideas to develop their own philosophies, which in turn would influence Jews centuries later during Hellenism.

If Solomon were as prolific a writer as the Bible claims, he may also have hastened the development of Hebrew into a newer style of language, and thereby differentiated himself from his contemporaries, making it harder for archaeologists to date his writings. If so, he could be comparable to Sir Francis Bacon around the time of the King James Bible (early 1600s), inventing English words and expanding its usefulness. Living languages evolve, and great thinkers who inhabit positions of influence often push their nations forward through literature and art. Solomon would have done that. By developing their own culture's language, leaders can update their nation's rhetorical tools, unlocking new ways of thinking, and entice foreigners. Solomon was clearly a researcher and student of wisdom, if he was anything at all.

THESE LOST TEXTS must have reinforced whatever we do find in Kings and Chronicles; it would make no sense for those texts to reference them otherwise. This means they affirm that Solomon was, at some point, extremely wealthy and powerful, and famous across the realm for his wisdom. And if these lost texts were written by true prophets, as we should assume, it means God felt the need to share extra information about him with Israel. We can't know why, but it must be. These would not be myths, fairy tales, or rumors about Solomon, but real accounts with God's stamp of approval.

Isn't it amazing to think that an assortment of respected, well-known, commonly available sacred texts—written by prophets!—were allowed to vanish into obscurity *after* the time of Babylonian captivity? This opens the door to any number of ancient texts being lost as well. It just so happens that we know about a few of them thanks to direct references in those few which survived! What if "The Visions of Iddo the Seer" also reference other books that we don't even know about? Should we really assume that these three scrolls happen to be the only important writings that disappeared? That hardly seems realistic. We should assume many writings are missing.

The very reason they became lost could be because everyone took for granted that they would never vanish from their archives. Nathan the Prophet, for example, was a contemporary of King David, so his writings must have been preserved for at least 500 years by that point! Iddo the Seer lived much later than Solomon, being the grandfather of Zechariah the Prophet (see Zechariah 1:7), and although he couldn't possibly have been alive at the time of Solomon, he was a "seer" and therefore might

164

have gained divine knowledge about Solomon from God directly.[62] Scribes may have considered it unnecessary to duplicate these scrolls precisely because they seemed so safe, intact, and valuable, which ironically doomed them to be lost completely when the time did come for them to vanish. It may have been inconceivable for them to be looted or destroyed by anyone; remember, Israel assumed that God would protect His people, and if not them, at least preserve His Word. The fact that God felt the need to produce these texts through His servants and even to cite them, but not to protect them in the end, challenges our entire view of scripture's role in God's plan.

Therefore, we have proof of the Bible's incompleteness *in the Bible itself.* These blank spaces might be enormous and contain critical data, leaving room for dangerous speculation. It means the Bible is partial and open-ended, not complete and closed. That's not something fundamentalists are prepared for. It should change the way we think about history, Israel, the Second Temple period, and God.

---

62 This also reinforces the traditional view that God gave certain prophets a download of historical data about things they had never witnessed, which speaks to the possibility of Moses knowing about Adam and Eve without having to rely on oral traditions or stealing from surrounding cultures.

WHAT GOD COULD DO

HAVING LOOKED AT A tiny sample of the language issues of the Bible—and I do mean a tiny sample!—the question of God's motives must be raised. Did He really want these kinds of arguments, misunderstandings, and conflicts? Doesn't it bother Him when people go to war over interpretations and so easily distort what He wants us all to place our trust in? Or, should we imagine that He cares a great deal, but not enough to take control of the situation? Is the fundamentalist's arrogance a real solution to all of this confusion, or are they making it worse and serving as an obstacle to a more sophisticated understanding? Do we have control over God's success or failure by the accuracy of our scholarship? That would be as shocking as anything we've looked at so far. In subsequent books I would like to address these questions more fully. For now, let me take a totally different approach to illustrating the issue.

Until now I have lamented the state of mankind, and that is proper. We know that billions are destined for Hell due to their (somewhat justified) doubts and ignorance about God's Word, and if we're realistic, we must say that this is God's fault. But what's more, I have lamented the tragedy of fundamentalism, because while it does not allow itself to doubt, it also does not engage honestly with the controversy, nor set a good example of searching out insight, which we are told so often in the Bible to do. And even if the fundamentalist approach is correct, this itself creates a paradox of "faithful denial" which is galling to those who hate confusion. But now I must change tactics and show you a different argument.

In my observation, people rarely understand the severity of a problem until somebody shows them what the alternative could be. Only then, after considering all the options that were available the whole time, the weirdness of "why" becomes felt at an instinctive level. If I am going to accomplish my goal of reducing cognitive dissonance in worship, I must demonstrate this. We will see that logic and history defy many of the doctrines held by traditional theology.

"God is not the author of confusion" (1Cor 14:33) and *"desires that all people are saved, and come to the knowledge of the truth"* (1Tim 2:4), but who are we kidding? If it were really so simple, things would have been very different all throughout history. Just how many billions of people have privately asked God to reveal Himself to them we can never know, but it's more than enough to have changed the trajectory of the whole world thousands of years ago if He had listened. I was guilty of this when I was younger, and many have confessed likewise. In fact, it's only natural to hear about God in your childhood and feel distant from Him as you get older, as if He does not care about your hardships, and when the Bible fails to fix this estrangement there comes a point where we pray for a sign. Why not answer?

For every person who feels like God has granted them a sign when they asked, there are thousands who were left wondering, or never even knew to ask. Jewish and Christian teachers alike dismiss the whole idea as untenable. They mock the idea that

God would personally reach out to every curious individual and persuade them to be faithful. But they don't have any logical arguments for why not. I will argue the opposite.

WITHOUT A DOUBT, GOD could personally reveal himself to humans individually and personally, and He has done so before! Not only is it possible, but He could do it in a way that would satisfy their skepticism and bypass any questions of language, which we know is a major problem throughout history, all the way back to the Tower of Babel. He knows everyone's hearts, and He knows what would suffice for them at that particular point in their lives. Could He do it for every human alive? Easily! We're talking about God, not a limited being.

Now there is a question of how this might look, and whether it would devolve into some bizarre state of civilization. Allow me to flesh out the picture more clearly, and make some suggestions for how God could have done it. As I picture it, there's no point in trying to arrange the parting of the Red Sea every few days, or gathering billions for a burning mountain, like Sinai. Great signs in heaven and earth are not necessary, although plenty of people who ask for a divine revelation want a miracle performed for them comparable to what's found in the Old Testament. That would be silly. My idea would work better.

Here it is in a nutshell: ***God could visit people in their dreams and teach them personally what they need to know.***

It's an elegant solution that only makes more sense as we analyze it. Every human being sleeps, and we all have dreams that impact our conscious mind already. These dreams don't seem to serve much purpose, and have often been misinterpreted by heathens and mystics. Dreams can feel more real than reality, however, and have no need to conform to physics or earhtly limitations. God could introduce Himself and explain the situation plainly, or trickle out clues a little at a time, from a young age. Even today, children have dreams which plant the oddest ideas in their subconscious. Fears and desires often form in their heads due to some combination of waking dissonance and dreams while they sleep, so why not use this valuable real estate (if we can think of it that way) for the ultimate communication system? That is not a rhetorical question.

COMPARE THIS IDEA TO what we got instead: the sporadic revelation of God's will to unexpected people, who almost universally failed to persuade their fellow countrymen and were killed instead, only to have their teachings written down and (we hope) preserved for later generations. It's absurd. Even major events in a small region won't make a difference a hundred miles away, and by the time the knowledge spreads it will be mingled with false reports, rumors, and local myths. If God wanted to send a message to the world, He could send it to the entire world over a 24-hour period while they slept!

We also know that the Holy Spirit is capable of miraculously imbuing a human being with profound spiritual knowledge.[63] Those who experienced these visions did not doubt them, because the Holy Spirit bypasses all rational thinking and simply grows their understanding at a critical moment in their lives, ensuring that they receive the help they need to become the person God wants them to be. In other words, God's power is not limited to natural phenomena and cosmic indications, but miracles can be performed *inside people's hearts*. They could wake up as improved people every day, not because they

---

63 See Elizabeth and Mary during their pregnancies, in Luke 1.

169

listened to some person talk about God or read from a book, but because they would have no choice. They would be confronted by God personally and develop a direct relationship with Him. And isn't that the whole idea?

For Almighty God to help people in their time of need with a strong message is aligned with what any good human father does for his children. We believe that God loves each of us, uniquely, seeing us individually as His children, and feels a profound sorrow when we stray from the right path. My solution would directly solve this paradox. We believe He is a God who never lacks awareness, never becomes tired, and that He has no problem giving people dreams and visions in order to alter their life, so why do we accept this juxtaposition so easily? Is it too much for God to be consistent?

My method would even double as a method of punishment and reward! This would reinforce God's moral standards clearly, leaving no room for endless arguments and misguided traditions. Not only would it be common to everyone, it would be impossible to ignore, and could even take a person on a journey of moral refinement as they got older and needed to learn more profound lessons!

It would work like this: if you've done wrong, you would go to sleep and have unpleasant dreams, if not nightmares, and then God (or an angel) could explain why exactly you are suffering that night, and how to avoid it next time. Jesus says that the angels that belong to children always face the Father in heaven (in Matthew 18:10), so why don't these same angels proceed to educate their little wards as they mature? Or, on the other hand, if you have listened and been good, you could have a blissful night of rest. You could have noble pleasures of the soul, and dream of something beautiful, acknowledging you for your good deeds, with divine encouragement. You would wake up feeling blessed and revived. How quickly these two consequences would correct a man's ways! With the imagination of God as the host of our dreams, the punishments and rewards would never get old. We know He can prepare eternal paradise, so He should be able to create the sort of dreams that make people love to obey.

There is nothing unreasonable about this method in terms of logistics or secondary effects. One person's dreams do not interfere with anybody else's, or with real life. It would leave no permanent damage or doom them for eternity. This allows them to repent and change their ways, which is the goal! They could be totally personalized, suited to the particular pathology of the individual, revealing their sinful thoughts to them, punishing them in some ironic way, or rewarding diligence and love. Such dreams could even include shared messages for entire groups, such as a family, town, region, language, or nation, so that they realize what they have in common. If everyone in a certain group experienced the same dream at the same time, nobody could deny the validity of what was said. There would be no more private disputes about what God wants! Skip the middle men, and give us the message directly. Today we have smartphones with satellite coverage around the world, and emergency broadcasts can be sent to billions of people at once, but God can tap into the unconscious mind anytime, anywhere. He can give us a regular update on what He wants, steering all the children toward life everlasting. That is truly loving.

Hypothetical example

A YOUNG MAN AND a bully go to school. The young man remembers some dreams about God when he was a child. These, he found, were consistent with what his friends and family have testified about themselves, so he is a believer who wishes to obey God. But as he goes to school, he is bullied and tormented by a classmate, who knocks him over the head with a thick textbook and pushes him down some stairs, causing a fractured elbow and a concussion. Fearing God and knowing the potential of what God can do, the young man does not retaliate, but only blesses his attacker, as Jesus would command.

That very night, the attacker goes to bed and thinks about the ways in which he was hurt by others, such as his older cousins, justifying to himself his actions as a form of passing along the pain, defying God's sense of justice. When he falls asleep, a dream takes over. In the dream, he is drifting on a raft in the middle of a great lake, alone. He calls for his family, but they are nowhere. He finds a paddle in the lake and begins to use it, but has little skill and nobody to show him how to use it. Then a bird swoops down and claws at him, scratching him for no reason. Then another, and another. He tries to hit them with the paddle, but they are always too agile and fly away. He becomes desperate but knows he can't swim, so he dares not jump in the water. Just then he sees another raft with the boy he attacked earlier that day, and that boy is not being attacked. So he knocks over the boy with the paddle, and climbs onto his raft, believing that this is the reason for the difference between them. But the birds only attack him twice as much, and knock the paddle out of his hand, which is taken by the boy in the water.

As the bully scrambles and slips off, he sees the other boy swim to his former raft and climb onto it. The birds do not attack him, but he calls out to God and a great wind carries him quickly to the shore on the other side, where God awaits. But for the bully, he begins to sink into the water, and tries to call out, but his head is going underwater, and he cannot make a sound. And so he sinks, desperate to cry for help but totally unable to. And in his last moments before he dies, he looks up and sees the light of God on the shore through the water, as bright as the Sun, and knows that it is not too late to call out, but in order to do so he must learn to swim and ignore the birds who attack for no reason. And so he wakes up.

The young man who was attacked also sleeps, and dreams of a painless reunion with God; the same God he remembers from his childhood, embracing him. He is told that he has done well, and that more rewards wait in the next life if he continues in this way. The joy he feels is incomparable, and it seems that hours go by with a hopeful sense that, as long as he does not grow bitter or avenge himself, God will defend him.

Would such a pattern not change the course of these young men's lives? How much more would it take than this, to cure every man of his ego, his angst, and his rebellion? This is only a mild version of what is possible with this solution, considering the power of God.

TODAY, THE ATTACKER COULD easily ignore the Bible's warnings, since it is considered a confusing and discredited work. This is thanks in large part to its strange history and language issues. Society can tell the bully anything about what's good and bad, justifying him with no divine intervention to set the record straight. Human punishments can always be turned into a personal conflict that only makes a pathology worse.

If the victim were attacked today, what would he think? Will he go to the scriptures and find a verse to comfort him? It is technically possible, sure. More likely he will allow the pain to fester, and pity himself. He will be angry at the unfairness, not knowing whether God cares or not. He might hear people speak confidently about a holy book that makes no sense to him. He would have trouble sleeping from the hurt elbow and, perhaps he gets told that he could die in his sleep from the concussion he suffered. So will he not hate God for allowing the wicked to prevail? Perhaps, if he does open the Bible, he will find Psalm 73, which speaks about similar situations this way:

> *But as for me, my feet had almost failed from under me – I was near to slipping – because of my envy of prideful men, when I saw the well-being of the wrongdoers. For they have no pain; their bodies are fat and strong. They are not in trouble as others are; they have no part in the unhappy fate of men. For this reason pride is around them like a chain; they are clothed with violent behavior as with a robe. Their eyes are bursting with fat; they have more than their heart's desire. Their thoughts are deep with evil designs; their talk from their seats of power is of cruel acts. Their mouth goes up to heaven; their tongues go walking through the earth. For this reason they are full of bread; and water is constantly flowing for them. And they say, "How will the Lord see this? is there knowledge in the Most High?" Truly, such are the sinners; they do well at all times, and their wealth is increased.*

174

*As for me, I have made my heart clean to no purpose, washing
my hands in righteousness. For I have been troubled all the day;
every morning have I undergone punishment.*

(Psalms 73:2-14)

Of course the psalm goes on to recognize the eternal doom of
the wicked, but the first part of the chapter expresses what the
ordinary person feels when they try to be good, not knowing
about any divine retribution. It doesn't have to be that way.

When approaching biblical problems, even the brightest scholars argue and undermine each other daily. I'm sure all of them
would find fault in my own tour of the issues. That is only to my
point, however, because I am not exactly stupid, and have tried
for years to listen to them already. If there is a grand answer I
am missing, I have only missed it because it is too obscure or
surrounded by confusion itself. In the next book I will bring up
many more objections of scholars and show how paradoxical
their own arguments become. The truth is, there is no unchal-
lenged authority in the world of Bible analysis. I can only feel
sorry for those who do not have the same time, access, or incli-
nations when they have questions of their own.

Just think how far we have come from fundamentalist assumptions in our little study. Rather than seeing the Bible as a
flawless work of divine autography (meaning God wrote it
personally) in a way that helps us understand His works and
requirements plainly, we have a maze of strange details and
historic influences creating a mess of everything. Even the
famous passages about divine inspiration do not say what
people think they say. Did Solomon write Ecclesiastes? Did Jesus
speak Aramaic? We should have solid answers to these

questions if God wants us to lean on Him for understanding, shouldn't we? When we understand how bewildering and divisive the Bible has become, let my suggestion of divine dreams stand as a contrasting option, showing that God had much different options.

Conclusion

SOMETHING IS WRONG WITH our theology, and more extreme fundamentalism does not seem like the solution. If we love our fellow man, let us reckon with what they're facing and not deny the issue. Faith is good, but to love your fellow man is the central command of the new covenant. Let us admit that God is at fault for what is happening, and we can either curse Him for not using His power to safeguard everyone, or radically change our perspective on what the Bible, history, and humanity is meant to accomplish.

Indeed, a paradigm shift of worship might be necessary, to include a lament, and sorrow, and a recognition of the paradox, while yet glorifying God. In some ways this is what King David, King Solomon, and the prophets Isaiah, Jeremiah, Ezekiel, and Daniel did before us, not to mention Moses. And Jesus was not thrilled with the arrangement he was put into either. Love compelled them all to lament from time to time, taking nothing away from God while acknowledging that He was responsible for the unspeakable conundrum of the world.

The fundamentalist claims to "fear God" as the Bible instructs, but what exactly is that fear? Is it only a reverence, as so many

Bible teachers and scholars agree? They have robbed fear of its anxiety, and turned it into mere respect. How many times have I heard Christians say that we should not really fear God, but only give Him honor! But that's not what I feel when I remove cognitive dissonance. What I feel on behalf of mankind is not just respect, but a dread for what God is capable of, knowing that the Almighty is willing to let billions of human souls descend into damnation for reasons we cannot decipher. Praise Him! Vanity of vanities – what can we do but lament and praise? The flames of Hell are not the creation of the Devil, but a place of righteous judgment, taking on God's very nature:

> *For the LORD thy God is a consuming fire, even a jealous God.*
>
> *(Deuteronomy 4:24, KJV)*

We can blame the Devil for many things, but he has no power that God did not give him. We can blame mankind, but we know His multitude of angels have intervened when it mattered to Him. We can blame ourselves for not understanding, but how can we understand anything without God opening our eyes and showing us the truth? God holds all the cards. He declares the end from the beginning. Fear Him as a dangerous force that can just as easily damn or save your soul. We are dust, and that even the greatest man is like a flower that fades quickly:

> *The LORD is lenient and gracious, slow to anger, and abundant in mercy. He will not always chasten, nor will He keep His anger forever. He has not dealt with us according to our sins, nor rewarded us according to our iniquities, for as the heavens are high above the earth, so is His mercy toward those who fear Him. As far as the east is from the west, so far has He removed our transgressions from us. As a father has compassion upon his*

children, so the LORD has compassion upon those who fear Him, for He knows our frame; He remembers that we are dust. As for man, his days are as grass; as a flower of the field, so he flourishes – for the wind passes over it, and it is gone; and its place will forget it.

But the steadfast love of the LORD is from everlasting to everlasting upon those who fear Him, and His righteousness is unto children's children, to those who keep His covenant, and to those who remember His precepts, to do them. The LORD has established His throne in the heavens; and His kingdom rules over all.

(Psalms 103:8-19)

If you believe the Bible, believe these words. Fear God with your whole heart, as if your life depends on it. What matters is timeless, and that is God's mysterious will, which we can only grapple with as Jacob wrestled with the Lord overnight, refusing to let go. Let us fear so that we submit, and let our submission generate an earnest pleading for answers, to help our fellow man. Do not hide your eyes from the sad state of the world when you sing His praises, but face Him as a child who knows not how to talk, or what to do. Give up on the rationalizations of modern theology, with their pleasant-sounding arguments, and say instead, "Woe to mankind! God has done this, and it is beyond our understanding!" From here, and only here, can we begin to absorb and internalize the tragic paradox.

Nevertheless, it is far too early to give up on answers. This is only the first study of the great paradoxes of God's reign, involving the most simple and obvious set of problems facing us as Christians. Fundamentalism is a flawed theological approach, but there are many other approaches with their own solutions to the fundamentalist's problems. In fact, many of the other approaches begin from this very point, at the realization that the text is not flawless and self-elucidating. Let us be willing to indulge them, to see what alternatives God has offered us. Because if God did not institute fundamentalism as we know it, He must have given us some other way of thinking about His Word. Nothing can change the facts of history, but we can at least align ourselves with the facts instead of setting ourselves against them.

If what I have said in this book is counted as foolishness, then I will go on to be a much greater fool yet, praising my God for all of our problems! What else should I do? How else should dust speak? If I am dust, then I will go on as dust, speaking to the Almighty about what it is to be dust! Far greater than I are His judgments, and terrible they are! You alone have instituted the absurdity, and granted dust to glorify You, Lord! You have given it a mind, not to understand, but only to sense in some profound way the paradoxes, and to painfully grope for answers without knowing in full:

> *For now we are peering as through a tinted glass, enigmatically; but then we will see face to face. Today I know partially, but in that day I shall know, even as I am known.*
>
> *(1 Corinthians 13:12)*

We should be of good courage. If we lament, we join the chorus of God-fearing men who lamented before us. Just as they proclaimed their faith despite what troubled them, with visions and mysteries too great to comprehend, we can also proceed with incomplete knowledge, as we do our part to steer the faithful away from arrogance and cognitive dissonance.

Throughout this book you will have noticed that scholars are the ones who refute fundamentalism, by pointing out problems in the texts, which opens the door to the Devil to sow confusion. But if scholars are the experts, do they really have the answers? How do they solve the paradox of the Bible? Often they leave their followers more confused and discouraged than they found them, and in the process expose their own biases. I still believe in the Bible, I believe in God, and I believe that there is a defense for Ecclesiastes being written by King Solomon, but it won't be as simple as fundamentalists prefer to believe. I believe we should face the research of scholars, the opposition of Atheists, and the questions of skeptics, but not stop there; we also need to question their motives and methodology in turn. The paradox of the Bible only goes deeper as we hear all sides of the story. For that, however, we will require another book.